OTHER BOOKS BY BILL YEARGIN

Yeargin on Management
What Would Dad Say? Now That He's in Heaven
Making Life Better: The Correct Craft Story

COMING LATER IN 2021

Education of a Traveler: Adventures in Learning Around the Globe

*To the wonderful people who have worked
beside me through both good and tough times—
to the degree I have enjoyed any success,
it is because of you, my teammates.*

Acknowledgements

To my cousin, thought partner, and editor Alex Gurtis. And, to Leigh. Your comments were all appreciated and made this book much better.

Table of Contents

Introduction: How I Got Here...

I am a CEO but, strangely enough, I never aspired to be one.

Yet, here I am. For the past fifteen years, I have been blessed to lead Correct Craft, in my opinion, the world's best organization and team. Many of my team members are smarter and more talented than I am. I hope they don't realize how much, but they likely do.

There are a million reasons why I should not be a CEO. I am self-deceived and can be easily fooled. For example, I sometimes feel one hundred percent right when I am actually one hundred percent wrong. I have a larger-than-normal number of relationships, but they don't tend to be deep. I can manage details when necessary but don't really like them. I can be overly analytical, which causes me to sometimes disregard the feelings of others, and I am generally impatient. Occasionally, I suffer from imposter syndrome, and other times, I get way too high on myself.

Fortunately for me, I have been exposed to numerous situations and experiences that have provided me a unique education as a CEO. I have visited over 110 countries, some of which I will discuss in my next book, *Education of a Traveler*. I have bought companies, sold companies, led turnarounds, and navigated organizations through both good times and bad. I have been privileged to study at some of the world's most respected universities, including Harvard, Stanford, and MIT, and I've met some of the world's most successful business leaders.

My insatiable desire to learn through reading has resulted in my consumption of innumerable business and leadership books.

I know the preceding paragraphs sound unbearably haughty, but I'm not writing them to praise myself. I am not claiming to be a great leader either, but I *have* had a great education in leadership.

This is the hardest chapter for me to write, and I would rather just leave it out, but some readers may want some background on me. I promise that the rest of the book is more interesting than this. If you know me well (or just don't care about my background), you might want to skip the rest of this chapter.

I grew up in South Florida, and I don't remember having career aspirations until middle school when I decided to become a pastor. I attended a small Christian school that gave significant affirmation to young men who wanted to become church leaders, and that seemed like the path for me. Later, in high school, I decided business was more to my interests, but I didn't understand what that meant other than a way to make money. Still, even in high school, I thought I might have a knack for it.

On my sixteenth birthday, I hit the job market and quickly landed a position as a bagboy with Pantry Pride, a local grocery store. I quickly learned that it only took four minutes from my day to punch in two minutes early and punch out two minutes late, and the extra four minutes made a big impression on the store bosses, who were used to dealing with teens milking the system in the other direction. I also learned that it's easier to be busy than to look busy. The seeds for both ideas had been planted by my dad, and for my first few weeks at the store, it seemed ridiculously easy (even for a sixteen-year-old) to impress the bosses.

Pantry Pride provided a lot of opportunities in the weeks, months, and eventually years ahead. Before graduating from high school, I was given the responsibility to manage the store two nights a week. My mom was proud to shop and see her son's name on the sign as night manager on Tuesday and Thursday nights. I thought it was pretty cool, too.

My high school years were exciting and fun, but I was not particularly focused on studying or becoming a stellar student. Lackluster study habits combined with a lack of desire to leave home resulted in me attending my local community college; it seemed to make sense. There, I met John Peterson.

John Peterson was a retired CPA (certified public accountant) who taught my accounting class at Palm Beach Community College. He had concluded a successful career and was giving back by investing in students like me. Mr. Peterson convinced me that the best way to ensure a successful career was to major in accounting. He said that as an accountant, I would never want for a job, and my accounting knowledge could be leveraged as a platform into any other area of business. He sold me, and from that freshman accounting class through the rest of college, I was determined to become a CPA.

As an aside, I deeply appreciate the investment John Peterson made in me, and I rarely refuse an opportunity to speak with college students, hoping I can inspire them too. Though I am not wired to be an accountant, I was a pretty good one. I quickly moved up the ladder, and accounting provided a great platform for my career and CEO education.

After completing my bachelor's degree in accounting at Florida Atlantic University, I was very fortunate, despite what I thought was a horrible interview, to land a job at the largest CPA firm in the world, Coopers & Lybrand. By twenty-one, I had graduated from college and was working for a great company. I was on my way.

I did have one huge hurdle, though. I needed my CPA license. At the time I took the CPA exam, it was a two-and-a-half-day test separated into four parts. Security was strict at the exam center and included bathroom monitors to make sure we were not cheating. It was a brutal three days, but after finishing the test, I planned to enjoy a weekend cruise with my friends who also took the exam. Nope—no cruise for us. I got home around eight p.m. the Friday night of the exam and slept until noon the next day; I was mentally and emotionally exhausted.

The exam could be passed in parts, and the first-time pass rate for all four parts at the time was about fifteen percent. I passed all four parts on the first try and was thankful because I could not imagine going through that experience again.

My Coopers & Lybrand years were brutal, and I consistently worked seventy to eighty hours a week. By twenty-three years old, I had been promoted to Senior Accountant and was running engagements at client sites. While I did not particularly enjoy my career at that time, it gave me invaluable business and leadership experience I could not have obtained anywhere else. In addition, mentioning I worked at C&L provided me instant credibility for much of my career, and I am thankful for the opportunity.

Knowing I wanted to work on my MBA as a path away from accounting, I left C&L after a couple of years of experience to work for a former client, Spencer Boat Company. This would provide me time to attend graduate school at night.

After getting my MBA, I took a short detour to work with a good friend of mine, Paul, at a holding company that owned multiple businesses, including the Breakers Hotel in Palm Beach. It was a fun job, and I loved the environment; I thought I would make a career there. Paul did make a career there, and for many years has been the company's CEO, for which I deeply admire him. However, Ed Bronstien, my previous boss who owned what was then known as the Spencer Boat Company (today known as Rybovich), came calling.

Ed Bronstien was someone I also deeply admired and a man who would become a second father to me. After I left Spencer Boat Company, he had acquired two other boat companies, and the industry had gone into a deep recession. Rybovich was in dire straits and losing money. Ed asked me to leave a secure career and come back to help turn the company around. At first, I refused, but he was persistent. Eventually, I reasoned that, being only thirty years old, I could always find another job if necessary, but an opportunity to use all the skills I had learned getting my MBA did not come along often—so I took it.

After going back to Rybovich, I quickly realized the company was in worse condition than I had understood. However, working closely with Ed's son, Jim, and others, we were able to turn the company around in less than two years. It was a stressful time but incredibly rewarding.

Word got out about the Rybovich turnaround, and I was invited to share our story at an industry conference in Newport, Rhode Island. I didn't realize it, but in the crowd was a publisher who needed someone to write a monthly leadership column for his magazine. The publisher invited me to fill that need, and while I was hesitant because I had never done anything like that, I decided to step out and try it.

Writing that monthly column had a huge impact on my career. I began getting invitations to speak all over the world, which gave me an opportunity to travel globally and meet leaders from many different backgrounds with differing perspectives. My thirties became a blur of working at Rybovich, writing columns, and traveling the globe to speak, often with one of my then-young daughters in tow because they were homeschooled.

After the turn of the millennium, Ed decided he wanted to sell Rybovich, so I worked with our bank to arrange a leveraged buyout that allowed his son, Jim, to acquire the business. Jim and I worked well together and had become good friends, so I was happy to help make this transaction happen. A couple of years after that deal, I worked with Jim again to sell Rybovich to one of the world's wealthiest families, the Huizengas of South Florida.

Not long after the sale of Rybovich to the Huizenga family, I was recruited to become CEO of Correct Craft but initially turned down the opportunity. I could not then imagine leaving my home in West Palm Beach. My family, my church, and my community service were all based in West Palm Beach, and I had what I thought were bigger plans, anyway. I was planning to leverage all the relationships and reputation I had built speaking around the globe and open a consulting firm. I did not aspire to be a CEO—instead, I wanted to work with many different organizations and offer my advice and experience.

I had hired a marketing advisor to help me open a new consulting firm, and we even recorded some videos to promote the venture when Correct Craft contacted me again. The company was going through a rough spell and could not hold onto a CEO. They had four CEOs in four years, and the gentleman who took the job when I walked away only lasted just over a year before leaving. This was not a cushy job.

After a series of signs and events I can only describe as divine, I decided to accept the Correct Craft position and become its fifth CEO in as many years. I moved my family to Central Florida and almost immediately regretted it. The company was a mess, but I believed I was meant to be there, so I stayed.

Our team at Correct Craft navigated a tough transition to new ownership and then had to manage through the 2009 Great Recession. It was excruciatingly difficult, but our team is amazing, and we did it.

We have grown from one location in Orlando to sixteen facilities around the United States, and we are now a global enterprise that sells its products in seventy countries. The organization is quite profitable, and in an industry with 35,000 companies, we have won almost every award, been recognized as the most innovative company, and were even named Florida's Manufacturer of the Year, which resulted in a visit from our state's governor.

Our success resulted from the most important lesson of this book, lesson one: "Be a learner." It's also truly amazing what you can accomplish with a great team, and that's exactly what we have at Correct Craft.

My years at Correct Craft have been exhilarating, and anyone interested in reading about them should pick up my book *Making Life Better: The Correct Craft Story*. (Or just buy one of our boats, and you'll get a free copy!)

Over the years, I have enjoyed an unusual opportunity to meet all types of leaders (some good and others not so good) and have spoken at meetings on every continent except Antarctica. This experience has provided me unusual access to the people leading organizations. I have been fortunate to spend time with business leaders, non-profit leaders, political leaders, and ministry leaders all around the globe, and I have tried to learn from them all.

I have worked with a man many consider the most successful entrepreneur ever—a man who became a multi-billionaire by having repeated success across many different industries—Wayne Huizenga. I have also been blessed to work with another successful business leader, Daryle Doden, who is breaking new ground by developing a philanthropic equity firm that will benefit many people for the next hundred years. I serve as a trustee of Daryle's estate and get to see firsthand the importance of making wealth matter through more than just consumption.

In addition to many unusual experiences, I have tried to be an academic learner. I read dozens of books a year and have attended some of the world's most prestigious universities to study business and leadership.

I have never focused on building a resume and have never postured or lobbied for jobs or titles that made it look like I was moving up. Honestly, over the years, I never thought much about building my career or becoming a CEO—until I was recruited to be one. Despite that, I have had an extraordinary opportunity to learn about leadership and what it takes to be a great CEO. (I'm not saying I *am* a great CEO. I know better than that.) However, I have learned a lot.

As you will read later in the book, I have always been passionate about developing those around me. I want to help people learn and am excited to share stories that are hopefully interesting and occasionally funny, but most importantly, I want to teach something. I want to help you be a better leader.

Let's get started.

FOUNDATION

Chapter 1

Be a Learner

During my fourth course at Harvard Business School, it was interesting to hear the professor begin the class with the Carter Racing case study. Unfortunately, I couldn't participate in the case study because this was my third time hearing it presented, and I knew about the surprise ending. However, knowing how the case was going to culminate gave me an interesting perspective as I watched my classmates wrestle with it.

My fellow students grappling with the case study were no slouches. They were ninety executives from all over the globe, many of them CEOs. However, despite their pedigrees, the case study progressed and concluded, predictably, exactly as it does when presented dozens of times each year at universities around the world.

In the Carter Racing case, students are required to make a decision between "Go" and "No Go" alternatives, and a high percentage of them initially choose to "Go." After the students have presented their decisions, the professor slowly releases more and more information that clearly demonstrates the correct decision is "No Go." On top of the analytical information that clearly demonstrates that "No Go" is the correct decision, the professor releases additional information that creates a strong emotional argument for the "No Go" decision. Finally, the professor concludes the case by presenting a linear regression analysis that demonstrates a ninety-nine percent probability that the "Go" decision is bad. At that point, the decision is simple, right? Not so much.

Each time I have seen the Carter Racing case presented, about ten to fifteen percent of the esteemed class continue to stick with their "Go" decision, even after hearing overwhelming evidence that it is a bad choice. It sounds crazy, but we, too, are all subject to those same blind spots. Most people prefer being a "knower" over a "learner." We all get trapped by our own perspective, but to reach your full potential as a leader, you must seek truth; you must be a learner.

In the book *When Prophecy Fails,* Leon Festinger demonstrates what often happens when events or information contradict what we believe—and we often double down on the wrong belief. The book presents research on groups that have predicted the end of the world on a certain date and how they reacted when the world did not end. Some of the group members will peel off, but it seems that there are always those who rationalize the failed prophecy and become even more entrenched, often setting a new date for the world's ending. In spite of the clearest evidence possible, people continue to hold onto their false beliefs.

In my next book, *Education of a Traveler*, I will share stories of visiting over 110 countries to demonstrate the benefits of being a learner. I have observed that while most people cling to being a knower, there is tremendous power in being a learner, and there are even a few classic books that help demonstrate this.

Gulliver's Travels

Gulliver's Travels by Jonathan Swift is the first-person account of Lemuel Gulliver, an English surgeon and sea captain who visits remote regions of the world.

Here's a brief overview of Gulliver's four trips:

- On his first adventure, Gulliver ends up on Lilliput as a captive of tiny people only six inches tall who are at war with another empire over which end of an egg should be broken first before eating it.

- His second adventure is to Brobdingnag where he is a tiny person in a land of giants many times bigger than him. He tells them about his country, England, and the giants are appalled by many things, including the idea of gunpowder and its use for hurting people.

- Gulliver's third adventure takes him to the flying island of Laputa where the people have interesting perspectives and plenty of what we would consider eccentricities, such as extracting sunbeams from cucumbers.

- His fourth and final adventure takes Gulliver to a land of super-smart horses called Houyhnhnms and not-so-smart people called Yahoos.

The book is a fun read, and I particularly enjoyed the reactions of the people Gulliver met on his travels when he shared with them how people from his home country viewed the world. The people Gulliver visited considered Western customs, many of which we still follow today, as absurd, and the reader can easily grasp their perspective.

As I recently finished re-reading *Gulliver's Travels*, I couldn't help but think of three major lessons:

1. **Get out of your comfort zone:** I know it's a cliché, but the lessons Gulliver learned were a direct result of him getting out of his comfort zone. My friend Michele Assad, who also happens to be an ex-CIA agent, often says, "Nothing impactful happens in your comfort zone."

2. **Be a learner:** *Gulliver's Travels* demonstrates how we can easily view other people's perspectives as absurd while they simultaneously consider our perspectives equally absurd. Very few people seek truth; most people seek validation of what they already believe. I found it interesting during the COVID-19 crisis to see how different people can look at the same exact data and make it fit into their preexisting narratives of the crisis. The same thing happens in politics when people celebrate something their politician did when they would condemn the same action if done by someone from another party. It is way

easier to be a "knower" than a "learner," but the best leaders are "learners." They seek truth, not confirmation.

3. **Pride is powerful and negative:** It takes humility to be a learner. Jonathan Swift ends the book with a speech by Gulliver decrying pride and the way it blinds people to instruction. Pride is dangerous because it keeps us from being learners when we really know very little. Several years ago, I read the book *Derailed* by Tim Irwin. In the book, Irwin reviewed the careers of several successful business leaders who lost their way. I remember thinking that downfall *always* comes back to pride. Every leader can be more successful by understanding and embracing the importance of humility.

Flatland

The depth of our self-deception is perfectly described in another classic book, *Flatland,* written by Edward Abbott during England's Victorian era. Abbott shares the story of a society that lives on a two-dimensional plane, appropriately called Flatland. We learn about Flatland from Square, who shares his story from prison. Square is in prison for revealing what he learned about a third dimension, which conflicts with the two-dimensional world the leaders of Flatland believe to be true.

The book also describes Square seeing Pointland, a universe occupied by its monarch, Point, who believes he is the entire world. It describes Lineland, a society that lives on a one-dimensional line, whose monarch wanted to kill Square after Square told him about the two-dimensional land where Square lives, a concept that seems impossible to the Lineland monarch. Finally, we learn about Spaceland, a three-dimensional world where Square first learns of a third dimension.

This story from Flatland may sound silly, but despite its grounding in Victorian views of classes and gender roles that are much different than today's, the book is thought-provoking and demonstrates how unusual it is for people to seek truth. We rarely seek truth but rather prefer validation. I've been down this road enough times to know that most people reading this book agree with me in general—they just don't see how the information personally applies to them. They are knowers, and in my experience, they can't conflict their already-held beliefs.

Being Wrong

In her great book, *Being Wrong*, Kathryn Schulz tackles this issue head-on. Schulz uses studies and anecdotes to explain why it is so typical and easy to feel one hundred percent right while in reality being one hundred percent wrong. Schulz uses example after example to demonstrate her point. The book was an eye-opener, and I highly recommend it.

It is a huge challenge to resist being a knower. As much as I understand this idea, and as many times as I have taught these concepts, I still struggle with it.

Thinking Fast and Slow

Nobel prize winner Daniel Kahneman explains this struggle in his book, *Thinking Fast and Slow*. Kahneman explains that at least ninety percent of our thinking is fast thinking, what he calls Type 1 thinking, where we draw quick conclusions based on our existing perspective. With Type 1 thinking, we use heuristics, or mental shortcuts, based on our worldview and other biases we have picked up over our lifetime. As we learn in behavioral economics, a science pretty much invented by Kahneman and his research partner, Amos Tversky, those heuristics and biases are notoriously wrong, even when they feel a hundred percent right.

In slow thinking, what Kahneman calls Type 2 thinking, we slow down enough to consider what we are trying to decide, but even then, we can be severely impacted by our biases. Like the people of Pointland, Lineland, and Flatland, it seems impossible that the world could be different than the way we see it. Speaking again of the book *Flatland*, remember the people of Spaceland, who live in the three-dimensional world like us? Once our friend Square became a learner, he asked the people of Spaceland about a fourth dimension, and they replied incredulously, just as Pointland, Lineland, and Flatland did when they were confronted with the thought of a new dimension. I am not a physicist, but that is something to think about, huh?

Do You Know the Way to the Moon?

When I think of the world's smartest non-academic organizations, NASA is at the top of my list. They are rocket scientists, literally.

Everyone reading this book most likely knows the story of NASA successfully responding to John F. Kennedy's 1961 challenge to land a man on the moon and bring him home safely. What you may not know is that NASA, too, can be subject to "knowing," and it almost resulted in not achieving Kennedy's goal.

Well before President Kennedy's challenge, NASA had been brainstorming different ways of landing a man on the moon and bringing him back, and there was one thing they "knew" for sure: Lunar Orbital Rendezvous (LOR) would not work. However, one engineer, John Houbolt, argued LOR was the *only* way to the moon.

The story of LOR and Houbolt is beyond the scope of this book, but, thankfully, NASA eventually shook away their knowing mentality and opened to the idea of LOR. The rest is history. On July 20, 1969, Neil Armstrong took the first step on the moon. The point is that even really smart people suffer from knowing, and it is likely that you do, too.

So, what can we do?

We can either approach life with a growth mindset or suffer the consequences of being a knower—and those consequences are high. Knowers stay trapped in their own thinking, which makes them feel good but also results in living a lie. They not only fail to reach their potential but also go through life deceived. Who wants to live with those consequences?

- **Acknowledge the reality of self-deception:** The first step to changing your world in a big way is to acknowledge the problem of self-deception. This is really tough for most people because they feel so right. For those who want to improve in this area, the books I mentioned above as well as those listed in the appendix will help.

- **Decide you would rather seek truth than feel good:** This too is hard because most people believe what they already think is truth, and it makes them feel good.

- **Surround yourself with people who will disagree with you:** Make sure your team knows you want their opinions, and never criticize, or, even harder, don't get emotional with someone for sharing their perspective in good faith.

- **Read material that broadens your perspective:** As you can already tell, I am a voracious reader, and I enjoy books that present a different perspective than my own. People will sometimes hear me share thoughts about a book and wonder why I would read something so different than my normal viewpoint. The answer is simple: I am not afraid of seeking truth, and that perspective has helped me materially over the years.

- **Travel to different places:** I have had the opportunity to travel to over 110 countries, and every visit to a different place expands my paradigms. You don't need to visit 110 countries, but try to visit someplace different; you will be surprised how your view expands.

- **Watch different news channels:** This point may be the toughest of all for some people. I am not a TV-watcher, but in the past few months, I have tried to watch different news programs, especially after a big event. The days of news programs sharing actual news are long over. They have become big echo chambers, and people listen to news channels that make them feel good about their views. Mix it up a little by watching something different.

There is tremendous opportunity to improve both yourself and your organization by being a learner. It is not easy, but once you start down the path, it is exhilarating. The number one thing that holds most people back in life is themselves, and, more specifically, their thinking. Being a learner will go a long way toward breaking free of self-deception and allowing you and your organization to reach your full potential.

Reflections

- It is possible to feel one hundred percent right when you are actually one hundred percent wrong.
- Most people go through life as "knowers."
- The only way to reach your potential as a leader is to go through life as a "learner."

Chapter 2

Feedback

I really disliked Janet at first, but later, I both respected and appreciated her.

As a recent, young college graduate working for Coopers & Lybrand (C&L) in the 1980s, life was frantic. I had a patient girlfriend (now my wife) and lived with my parents, so there was a lot of time to focus on work. My willingness to do whatever was asked of me paid off, as I was assigned to the office's plum clients, becoming someone the bosses wanted on their teams.

I was disappointed several months into my time at C&L when I was assigned to a municipal client with Janet, a senior accountant who had recently been transferred into our office. Government work did not interest me, and Janet came with a reputation of being challenging, but it was for just a few weeks. I figured I would be back to the primo for-profit clients I preferred after a small speed bump on the fast track of my career. Then Janet gave me a surprise: a mediocre evaluation.

At C&L, staff accountants were frequently moving from one job to the next and working with different senior accountants who ran the jobs on-site. After every job, we would get a formal performance evaluation, which resulted in a dozen or more evaluations each year. Up until Janet, my evaluations had been exemplary. Janet's evaluation of me was not bad, but it also was not consistent with the great evaluations I was used to receiving. I thought she was trying to torpedo my career.

Normally even-keeled, I was downright irritated at Janet, and unfortunately, because of my immaturity at the time, I stayed that way for the rest of my career at C&L. Now I understand that Janet was doing me a favor and trying to help me. Janet, if you read this, please call me!

I know now that I need feedback. I am self-deceived. I feel a hundred percent right at times when I am actually a hundred percent wrong. I have blind spots; I get emotionally hijacked, and I don't know what I don't know.

I Need Help!

Every other year, I ask our team at Correct Craft to do a 360-degree evaluation of me, and at other times, I ask my direct reports to each give me ways I can be a better leader. I very much want to improve and know I need feedback to do that. Where better to get feedback than from those who are closest to me?

We all want feedback when it's good. However, it's our natural inclination to dismiss negative feedback, especially if it conflicts with our self-identity. Our self-perception is powerful and hard to overcome. In fact, we can find plenty of reasons to dismiss constructive criticism, and it is especially easy to do if we are the boss.

Our self-identity is strong. We tend to attribute our own failures to circumstances, while others attribute them to our lack of competency, chemistry, or character. We discount how our emotions impact others, while those around us magnify them. Often, we judge ourselves based on our intentions, while others judge us based on our actions.

Everything I have written above is true about me, and it is about you, too. Feedback is often hard for people to give us, even when we ask for it. And if you are the boss, there is a good chance that you have no clue about your real opportunities to improve.

Fortunately, there is an easy fix for this problem. If we can get beyond the insecurity of feeling a loss of control or having our self-identity threatened, there is tremendous value in receiving feedback from others. It can make us all significantly more effective, as long as we are open to listening.

Some ways you can get and use feedback to improve both your personal and organization's results are as follows:

- **Acknowledge the value of feedback:** If you are using your position as a boss to discourage or deflect feedback, it is leadership malpractice, and you are hurting yourself, your organization, and your team.

- **Ask for specific feedback:** As I mentioned above, every other year, I ask our team to give me a 360-degree review, and recently, I asked them each for two ways I could improve. I understand that it is hard for many people to give their boss negative feedback, so it is the boss's responsibility to make sure their team is comfortable doing so.

- **Work to understand the feedback:** You do not have to agree with the feedback, but understanding it will go a long way toward helping you learn about opportunities to improve. Most leaders will have a hard time understanding feedback, but the more uncomfortable it makes you, the more there is to learn.

- **Make changes:** Find something in the feedback you can change to be a better leader. If you cannot find anything, either you have not created the right environment for your team to provide feedback, or you are not working hard enough to understand it.

- **Respond to the feedback:** If you ask those on your team for feedback, be sure you let them know you have considered it, and if there are changes you plan to make, let them know that too. Most importantly, do not discount the feedback or get defensive. How you react to feedback will significantly impact how your team responds next time you ask for it. It also models how they should receive feedback as well.

Anyone who has read my books or articles or has heard me speak, knows the importance I put on being a learner. Being a learner helps leaders in many ways, both professionally and personally. An important part of being a learner is accepting feedback.

Ohio State Buckeyes and Uber

A few years ago, my son-in-law Ben and I flew to Columbus to watch an Ohio State football game. We were guests of Ohio State coach, Urban Meyer, which meant we had sideline passes, access to a suite with a great view of the game, and delicious food. This included unlimited buckeyes, which are a chocolate-and-peanut butter delight. I don't want to think about how many calories I consumed in the form of buckeyes that night.

Game weekend, we stayed near the airport, which is about a ten-mile drive to the stadium. Big mistake. On game day, we decided to Uber into the campus to join the 102,000 people attending the event. Another mistake. Though we left the hotel a couple of hours early to be safe, the traffic was horrendous. This was partly because many roads to the Horseshoe (Buckeye fans will understand) seemed to be unnecessarily closed, which only made the situation worse.

In what seemed to be a painfully bad example of traffic management, vehicles, including our Uber, were directed about a mile past the stadium to turn around and come back the same mile to the stadium drop off area. Stop and go traffic—mostly stop—on the highway was frustrating, especially since the stadium was only a few hundred yards away from where we sat in our Uber. That's when I got a great idea: Jump out of the Uber on the highway and walk to the stadium. This was the worst mistake of the trip.

Just as we were jumping out of the car, a policeman from seemingly nowhere yells at us to get back in and orders the Uber driver to pull over. The Uber driver was given a ticket for illegally discharging passengers on a highway, despite my pleas to the policeman that it was my fault, not his. My mistake was now getting expensive.

Despite a colossal mess, the Uber driver continued to be nice and drove us to the drop-off area before leaving us with an, "Enjoy the game, go Bucks!" It was not just this driver who was nice when he should have been mad at me. I have hired dozens (likely more) of Uber drivers, and while most of the rides are less dramatic than that one in Ohio, the drivers are always nice. Do you know why? Feedback, a.k.a. ratings. Feedback is powerful.

It is interesting to consider that the feedback Uber drivers receive have changed the taxi industry. I have been in hundreds of taxis over the years, and there has been a noticeable improvement in the cab driver's attitude since Uber started offering rides. Some say it is competition, which is correct when it comes to the big picture. However, the taxis are competing with Uber drivers who are being extra nice.

Feedback has done what many would have said was impossible: It turned grumpy cab drivers nice. For the record, I did ask the driver in Ohio for his address and mailed him money for the ticket. And I just checked my own Uber rating while writing this, and it was 4.96. If you were wondering, I am normally a great Uber passenger.

Feedback is an underutilized superpower. It is hard on the giver and even harder on the recipient, but if done constructively, it can be incredibly beneficial.

If you are interested in exploring the topic of feedback further, I highly recommend the book *Thanks for the Feedback,* which was written by Harvard professors Douglas Stone and Sheila Heen. I learned a lot from this book. The authors claim that nothing impacts a learning organization more than the way its executive team accepts feedback. If you want your team to accept feedback and to learn and grow, you need to model it.

Feedback is a simple and inexpensive way to significantly improve both yourself and your organization. I know I need help, and so do you!

Reflections

- Feedback is often hard to both give and receive.
- There may be no other way to see our blind spots than to embrace feedback from our team.
- We need to create an environment where people are comfortable giving feedback.
- Healthy feedback can transform you and your organization.

Chapter 3

Vision

Where there is no vision, the people perish. —Proverbs 29:18

Wayne Huizenga was not a one-trick pony. He made billions of dollars in industries as diverse as garbage collection, car sales, video rental, hotels, and professional sports teams. Wayne had incredible and repeated success in different industries partly because he had great vision. I didn't work closely with Wayne, but I did have the opportunity to be in several meetings with him and was always impressed. He had the ability to see things others could not.

One day in my West Palm Beach office, I received a call from Wayne's assistant, Sonya, asking me if I wanted to join him on a trip to South Africa. Wayne co-owned a home with Gary Player and Jack Nicklaus on the edge of Kruger National Park, which he wanted to visit, and he asked me to join him. The trip overlapped by a day with a visit to Aruba I had planned with my wife, Leigh, but, being a good sport, she agreed we would come back from Aruba a day early so I could travel with Wayne to Africa.

We flew to South Africa in one of Wayne's private Boeing Business Jets (BBJ). Think full-size commercial passenger jet but outfitted to transport about a dozen people in incredible luxury. Interestingly, at the time, Wayne had two BBJs, plus several other jets, seaplanes, and helicopters. Spending several days up close with such a brilliant leader was a unique experience.

There were a handful of others also on the plane, but for takeoff and our first couple hours in the air, I had the opportunity to sit with Wayne. Hearing him talk about his career and having the opportunity to ask about some of his incredible accomplishments was a wonderful experience. Wayne's vision was extraordinary, and I believe it was one of the primary reasons for his success. He clearly saw opportunities and solutions to problems that others couldn't, and it was the closest I have been to experiencing a savant. Wayne's vision was that good.

Some people have great vision naturally and, in my opinion, it was a wonderful God-given gift that Wayne enjoyed. Fortunately, as we will see, for those of us who do not have a Wayne Huizenga-like vision, there are still things we can do to improve.

Vision in Ethiopia

Visiting Ethiopia, I saw firsthand the work of a couple with incredible vision via Demi and Marta, founders of Project Mercy. I met Demi and Marta at a conference in Austria, where they invited me to bring a team of employees from our company to help them in Ethiopia. A trip like this was not unusual for our team, and in *Education of a Traveler,* I devote an entire chapter to our company's service work. I will also touch on it later in this book's "culture" chapter. As part of Correct Craft's service initiatives, I was happy our team could help Demi and Marta in their work.

In the 1970s, Demi and Marta were Ethiopian refugees fleeing for their lives, literally, from the Marxist government then in power. Fortunately, they escaped to Kenya before being sent to the U.S. as refugees. They were on the run but loved their country and had great vision.

After settling in the United States, they began raising money to assist fellow refugees and were able to help many destitute Ethiopians who struggled for survival. Eventually, they were allowed back into Ethiopia and they settled in Yetebon, a primarily Muslim community that was the birthplace of Marta's father. Once in Yetebon, the community elders asked Demi and Marta to help them educate their children, since education, and particularly speaking English, was viewed as a ticket to help their kids out of extreme poverty.

Driving the two hours from Ethiopia's capital, Addis Ababa, to Yetebon, our team felt like we were in a time warp. We rode through communities that looked like they had not changed for 2,000 years, and, to be fair, they probably hadn't. The community of Yetebon was the same way, with many of the people we met there living in stick huts with zero modernity. It was clear to see, though, that Demi and Marta's vision was *transforming* Ethiopia, and I don't use that word lightly.

What Demi and Marta had started as an organization to help refugees, and then transitioned into a school in Yetebon, has blossomed into a catalyst for transformation (there's that word again) in the country. Our team saw all kinds of catalytic work being done by Demi, Marta, and the Project Mercy team. They had set up a feeding program, adult education, and job training, while also becoming a healthcare provider, including helping with HIV/AIDS education. We also saw the Project Mercy team working hard to help Ethiopians provide for themselves by teaching agricultural methods, including the use of irrigation systems.

Our team was blown away by what Demi, Marta, and the Project Mercy team had done in Ethiopia—and that's an understatement. Project Mercy's work does not just happen—Demi and Marta had a wide and clear vision, and, with a great team, executed it well.

Leaders Rarely Go Further Than Their Visions

As a CEO, requests to join various boards come my way frequently and, for various reasons, I rarely accept. Besides serving as a board member on a plethora of Correct Craft organizations, as I write this, I am also serving on the board of the National Marine Manufacturers Association, an organization I am happy to help, as they have a huge positive impact on our industry. However, there is one very unusual organization where I also serve as trustee: the Doden Legacy Trust (DLT).

The DLT is an innovative entity that is the brainchild of Daryle Doden and is set to manage the assets of Daryle and his wife Brenda for the next one hundred years, way past their deaths. Daryle's DLT concept is innovative because it is designed to invest in organizations that will drive culture in the marketplace, like we try to do at Correct Craft. The DLT also invests (a deliberate word choice) its profits, and eventually the corpus, in philanthropic endeavors.

The details of the DLT are beyond the scope of this book, but, wow, what vision! Daryle wanted to create a vehicle to invest his and Brenda's assets to make a difference in the marketplace and philanthropically, not just to be given away at death. Based on what I can tell, Daryle has created something not done before. That takes vision in spades.

Vision has impact. If you can expand yours, it will have a dramatically positive impact on you and your career.

To some, including Wayne Huizenga, Demi and Marta, and Daryle Doden, vision is a God-given gift. Best I can tell, they were born with it and used it wisely. Wayne helped a lot of people through business, and Demi and Marta are helping Ethiopians in a variety of ways. Daryle is breaking new ground on how wealth can be stewarded.

But what about those who don't have natural vision? Fortunately, there are things we can do to improve.

- **Value other perspectives:** When I was traveling a lot to speaking events, I almost always brought with me a deflated beach ball. I would inflate the beach ball and bring it into the meeting while asking people to imagine it was the world and they were standing on one of the colors. Whatever color they were on was how they viewed the world, while others saw the world through the lens of their color. The best leaders try to see all the colors of the beach ball. It's funny, but even now when I speak at conferences, someone will inevitably come up to me and ask, "Do you still use the beach ball?"

- **Get a view from the periphery:** Disruptive innovation rarely comes from an existing player in an industry, or if it does, they often ignore the opportunity and fail to monetize it. Often the exceptional (i.e., disruptive) ideas come from outsiders who are not captured by the current way of thinking. Working to get this outside view will go a long way toward improving your vision.

- **Think crazy big:** Develop your ideas exponentially until they feel impractical or even like a waste of time. This will help you see alternatives that you might not have considered.

- **Don't be trapped by the past:** The business landscape is littered with companies that were trapped in the past, and it destroyed them. Think Kodak, Palm, Nokia, Blockbuster, and many others. The past is a trap that is hard to escape, but awareness of it is the first step toward not falling prey.

- **Get outside your comfort zone:** Stepping into uncomfortable situations is a pillar of being a learner. Your comfort zone can only be expanded by stepping out of it.

- **Focus on results, not activity:** We will discuss this later in the book, but focusing on activity over results is one of the biggest snares that keep leaders from reaching their potential. Activity limits vision.

- **Be a learner:** Are you picking up on a theme? We need to seek truth, not validation. Read books and meet with people who see things differently than you. Travel to new places. Watch a different news channel. When your mind is changed on a topic, celebrate. Be a learner.

Several years ago, while attending a charity auction for the high school I attended, I bought a hot air balloon ride for me and my mother to enjoy. A hot air balloon ride was on my bucket list, and I was pretty sure it was something Mom would like as well, so I decided to splurge and pay more than I should have, knowing the proceeds were going to a good cause.

We scheduled our trip for a sunrise takeoff in Fort Lauderdale, about an hour south of where I lived in West Palm Beach. After a short set of instructions, the pilot fired up the balloon, and we took off. It was breathtaking. We soared through the South Florida sky with a chase car, since we were not exactly sure where we would land. Mom still says it was one of the highlights of her life.

After about forty-five minutes, the pilot started scoping out potential landing sites and, with the help of the chase car crew, identified one in a public school field downwind of our path. As we got closer to the field, the pilot reduced the heat in the balloon, which started lowering us over a neighborhood on our way to the landing spot. We eventually landed safely and celebrated a great experience.

Besides having fun, that hot air balloon ride impacted my perspective. As we rode over that neighborhood, seemingly less than a hundred feet off the ground, we saw the homes and people from an unusual viewpoint. Dogs barked at us, and people in their yards enjoying their morning coffee and paper looked up at us in surprise. It felt a little uncomfortable, even mildly voyeuristic, to have our perspective from the balloon. It felt like we were seeing this neighborhood and its people from a perspective few ever do.

One key to effective leadership is seeing things from a bigger picture by expanding your view or vision. The French novelist Marcel Proust said that "More important than seeing new lands is seeing familiar ones with a new set of eyes."

Reflections

- Leaders are limited to the extent of their visions.
- A broad vision contributes to success.
- There are specific things we can do to expand our vision.

Chapter 4

Mindset

If you think you can, you will. If you think you can't, you won't.

My third year in college, I was living in the dorms at Florida Atlantic University when I went through a phase of reading self-improvement books. It was during this time that I picked up *Psycho-Cybernetics,* by Dr. Maxwell Maltz, a classic book that changed my life. It was written in 1960 and is still in print today.

Some might call *Psycho-Cybernetics* "hocus pocus." I understand why folks might be skeptical of the book, but it helped me understand how much our mindset impacts both our effectiveness and our success. *Our success is as impacted by how we think as much as it is by our skills.* Please read that last sentence again and think about it. People who don't understand this can go through their entire lives wondering why they are good at what they do but it does not bring them the success they desire.

There are a handful of my friends (you know who you are!) who always ask me what I am reading and what I have learned since we last met. Sometimes when we're going to speak or meet, I think ahead about what I'm currently learning because they will ask. These friends are exhilarating to be around, and I love hearing about great books they have read and what they've learned, too. They have a growth mindset.

The idea of a growth mindset is explained clearly by Carol Dweck in *Mindset,* her aptly named book. Dweck differentiates between people who have a "growth" mindset or a "fixed" mindset. You can likely guess which one tends to be more successful.

Most people have a fixed mindset, but they don't realize it. In fact, it is almost impossible for someone with a fixed mindset to realize it. According to Dweck, here are a few ways that we can identify our mindset:

- A growth mindset embraces challenges; a fixed mindset avoids them.

- A growth mindset persists; a fixed mindset gives up easily.

- A growth mindset sees effort as a path to mastery; a fixed mindset discounts effort.

- A growth mindset learns from criticism; a fixed mindset avoids it.

- A growth mindset gets inspiration and learns from the success of others; a fixed mindset feels threatened.

In our Correct Craft-owned businesses, we have seen a direct correlation between leaders who have a growth mindset and success. Having a growth mindset is powerful.

I suggest many books, but Dweck's *Mindset* is near the top of my recommendation list. Leaders who get their mindset right find that everything else comes easy.

Move Toward Problems

A friend of mine, Michele Assad, is an ex-CIA agent and author of *Breaking Cover*. It's always interesting to hear stories from her CIA days. One thing I have enjoyed hearing Michele talk about is how the CIA teaches its agents to respond to trouble. She shares the idea that challenges put us on an X with three choices: fight, flee, or freeze (stay on the X). According to Michele, the CIA teaches its agents that there are times to fight and there are times to flee, but you ALWAYS "get off the X."

One way to get off the X is to take ownership of the challenge.

It is impossible to be a great leader without a) taking ownership of challenges and opportunities, b) being decisive, and c) being willing to be held accountable for results. That all seems easy until a new leader must actually do those three things. Often, there is staggering pressure that comes with responsibility and accountability, especially when decisions impact many people's lives.

I have seen leaders who distance themselves from challenges when it seems like the challenges may not end well. Often those leaders are trying to be subtle, but what's happening is almost always crystal clear—the pressure is on, and they are afraid of failing and what the personal consequences might be. Poor leaders distance themselves from challenges, but exceptional leaders double down when challenged. They fully engage, take responsibility for the situation, and make it right.

It takes a unique person to move toward challenges and not distance themselves from risk. My experience is that introverts have a tougher time moving toward challenges than extroverts. Extroverts often see their environments as smaller than them. Introverts are the opposite; they see themselves as smaller than their environments. But regardless of your wiring, to be a successful leader, you must take ownership, even when the odds are long.

My first two days at Correct Craft were eye-opening. I knew there were problems that needed my attention as the company's fifth CEO in five years, but I did not realize how dire the situation was when I arrived. After the second day, our now-owner Daryle took me aside and asked if I was going to be okay, to which I replied, "I may get fired, but I am going to make the necessary decisions to get us through this." I have heard Daryle tell that story many times over the years, and he always concludes by noting that the moment he heard that, he knew Correct Craft would be okay. I was taking ownership.

What Can You Control?

I have both read and recommended Steven Covey's masterpiece, *7 Habits of Highly Effective People,* countless times. If you have not yet read *7 Habits*, drop this book now, and go get yourself a copy. It's that good.

Covey writes a lot about mindset, and one of the most powerful concepts he highlights is the importance of focusing on what we can control. So often, we spend our time wondering or worrying about what someone else is doing, or any other thing we cannot control, including the weather. It's a waste of time. People who reach their potential don't waste time focusing on things they cannot control; they are laser-focused on what they can impact.

Management guru Peter Drucker has said, "There is no greater waste than being good at something that does not matter." Otherwise phrased as: *More important than doing things right is doing the right things.*

Most leaders want to feel busy because they equate busyness with results, but that's wrong. Read that sentence again, it's important. There is zero correlation between busyness and results.

I would much prefer the leaders at our company work thirty hours a week and get great results than work eighty hours with lesser results. In fact, working more hours for lesser results is a pretty clear sign of a poor manager.

The most successful leaders have a results-oriented mindset.

If a leader is not sure how to get results or have an impact, they make themselves feel important by being busy. Often, this includes doing things that they should not even be doing. The best leaders avoid this trap.

So why do leaders place busyness over impact? Basically, it makes them feel better. It makes them feel important, and they love to tell people how busy they are. Breaking out of this trap will exponentially improve a leader's performance.

See Problems as Opportunities

As I have written earlier, when I assumed my current CEO role, our company was in a mess. The first couple years in my new role were spent putting out fires, trying to develop long-term strategies, and navigating a company ownership change. Then, just when things seemed to be on track—one month after we completed the sale of our company and literally on my second anniversary—the bottom of the economy fell out, and we entered the Great Recession.

The Great Recession was excruciatingly difficult on our company. We lost ninety percent of our business seemingly overnight. However, it also helped us create a foundation that resulted in a decade of record-breaking results. This foundation was laid because we were able to make several years' worth of improvements to our business in a matter of weeks.

Leaders should view problems as an opportunity for a significant reset of their businesses. Challenges, such as what we have gone through with COVID-19, are rare opportunities to restructure our businesses in a way that benefits our teams for the next decade.

Specifically, in tough times, think about how you can change your business for the better—then do it. You need to be sure that after the first crisis, your business has processes and a cost structure that produces better results when the next one hits.

For instance, are there things you stopped doing during the crisis that you do not need to restart? Or can you reduce the number of resources needed for a particular job or function? Are there processes that would be tough to change in normal times that might be easy to change during a crisis?

Challenges, and even crises, present leaders an opportunity they may never get again. It is an opportunity to make changes to ensure your organization's long-term health. Making changes takes energy and courage, but crisis offers the opportunity to make your business much better. If you take the opportunity, your employees and company will benefit from it for the next decade.

We learn a lot about ourselves and each other in times of crisis, and it takes an exceptional leader to not only recognize and grow from what they are learning, but to also look for opportunities to improve.

Humility

Humility is, perhaps, the most critical mindset for a leader. Sometimes that can be hard because leaders enjoy when people laugh at their jokes, act happy when they walk in a room, and generally want to please them. It is easy for leaders to become prideful, but over and over again, I have seen that pride is the root of leadership destruction.

Tim Irwin explains this well in his book *Derailed.* In *Derailed,* Irwin looks at the careers of several "rockstar" CEOs whose careers got off track (i.e., derailed). In each case, they were leaders who seemed to have it all, the proverbial golden touch, but eventually, it all came crashing down. Irwin identifies multiple reasons for the downfall of these CEOs, but the root cause was pride.

When leaders start feeling as though they're special or don't need outside input, those are early warning signs of a pride problem. These warning signs are indications that you could be wrong. When a leader starts feeling smart or special, watch out; there may be a derailment on the way.

Pride feels so darn good, but we must be smart enough to see beyond it.

Reflections

- *How we think* is often more important than *what we do*.

- The best leaders have a *growth mindset*.

- Leaders should *move toward problems*, not look for ways to distance themselves when things get tough.

- Focus on *what you can control*.

- Don't fall into the "activity" trap—focus on results instead.

- *Problems* are often huge *opportunities*.

- To avoid being "derailed," stay humble.

Chapter 5

Integrity

An entire life is often measured by one bad choice.

Most people love their fathers, and of course, I love mine too.

Growing up was special at the Yeargin house in Palm Beach Gardens, Florida, first on Keating Drive and later in the same neighborhood on Crestdale Street. My brother, Doug, and I had wonderful parents who were fully engaged in our lives. They were at all our sports events, often with my dad as the coach, and they never missed a speech, play, concert, or anything else in which Doug or I participated.

Even in our adult years, Mom and Dad were fully engaged in our lives. Well after my father was on disability for Parkinson's disease, he enjoyed spending time with us and his grandchildren. Unfortunately, dad's diagnosis resulted in his early death, and the toughest period of my life were the last two weeks of his. I spent day and night with him in our local hospice center.

I won't give away her age, but fortunately, we still have Mom with us. She is a huge blessing to both Doug and me as well as her six grandchildren and their spouses.

Dad was the highest example of integrity I have known. In the thirty-seven years I had with Dad, I cannot recall him ever even getting close to compromising his integrity. He was the kind of guy who would drive back to the store if the cashier gave him a few cents too much change. Dad was straight-up honest, and his word was better than any contract.

As I have thought back on Dad's life, I don't remember even one instance of him exhibiting hubris or holding himself out for praise or recognition. He was a humble man with high integrity who was trusted by everyone who knew him. If I am half the man he was, I have hit a home run.

Correct Craft

Without digging too deep, anyone can find examples of extreme integrity in the history of our company, Correct Craft. Indeed, it was one of the things that attracted me to the company. I wrote about some of the Correct Craft stories in my book, *Making Life Better: The Correct Craft Story*, and if you're interested in reading about a very unique company and how it has led an industry with integrity for nearly one hundred years, please pick it up. Or, as I mentioned earlier, buy one of our boats, and you will get a copy for free!

Probably the most unique story in Correct Craft's history of integrity is the story of its bankruptcy. I tell the story in detail in my previous book, but below is the short version.

Things were going well for the company when Correct Craft received a government contract in 1957 for 3,000 fiberglass assault boats. The work was proceeding smoothly with the contract until a corrupt government employee delivered a veiled request for a payoff through double reimbursement of his expenses. Basically, he wanted a bribe.

The company refused the inspector, even though it would have been a small cost related to the total government project, and that's when the fateful slide toward bankruptcy began.

In retaliation, the government employee began rejecting boat deliveries, and Correct Craft didn't receive payment for boats that, in their judgment, were perfectly sound. At one point, eight out of ten boats were disapproved. Rejected boats piled up in the storage yard.

Then came the final blow. A flatcar had just been loaded with forty previously passed boats. The government employee appeared suddenly, just as the switch engine backed up to the flatcar. Pointing to the boats, he said he didn't like their looks and that they should be unloaded and refinished.

That arbitrary decision, unfair as it was, made it impossible to continue. The contract had already cost the company $1 million more than it had received, and Correct Craft now owed half a million dollars to 228 creditors. Furthermore, the bank had withdrawn all of its commitments. In dire straits, they filed a complaint with the Army Corps of Engineers in an attempt to collect on expenses owed them under their contract, but to no avail.

After considering one more time if they should just pay the bribe, the company decided that was not the right thing to do and was left with only one choice: bankruptcy.

As the bankruptcy proceeded, creditors ended up accepting ten cents on the dollar. It was a discouraging time for the company and its owners, the Meloon family.

As time passed, the Meloons couldn't rest without paying back the remaining debt to every single one of the 228 creditors. The family spent the next couple of decades locating and repaying each one the full amount they owed until the entire debt was settled in 1984. By all accounts, it wasn't easy to find all the creditors, and when one died, Correct Craft spent time searching for the nearest relative and paid them.

Today, nearly forty years after the last creditor was paid, I still have people tell me they want to do business with us or buy one of our boats because leaders of our company, when I was still just a kid, made the decision to act with integrity.

Not Only Right, but Smart

Should we demonstrate integrity because it is the right thing to do? Absolutely.

Is it also smart business? Yep, it is.

My uncle Wilbur was a bit of a living legend as I was growing up. During our family visits to Oxford, North Carolina, where my father's family lived, he seemed like the king of the town. The quintessential entrepreneur, he was a tobacco farmer, owned a warehouse, sold fertilizer, and had a realty company and a bunch of other little businesses in the community. While he certainly could afford something nicer, he always drove a twenty-year-old sedan covered with red dirt picked up driving through his tobacco fields.

The best part is that Uncle Wilbur was a handshake guy. I am sure he had some written contracts, but everyone knew his word was gold. His integrity was why people wanted to deal with him and played no small part in his extraordinary success.

We see the same thing today as we acquire companies at Correct Craft. We have tried to build on the integrity our company has shown over the decades, and sellers respect that. They know we will take care of their brand, legacy, and employees long after they are gone. And they know that what we say is more than just words—we have a track record that demonstrates that we do what we say. Over the last decade, we have been able to execute the best acquisition deals in our industry because we have a reputation of integrity.

Taking short-term losses because of your integrity almost always comes back to benefit you in a big way. Companies that have the strongest foundation and are the most successful in the long run are built on integrity. It's the reason Correct Craft is heading toward its one-hundredth anniversary.

Motivation

As I wrote the "Not Only Right, but Smart" section above, I was feeling a lot of tension. I don't want people to read it and think they can fake integrity in order to manipulate others. Motivation matters.

Nobody explains this better than Patrick Lencioni in his great book, *The Motive*. In *The Motive,* Lencioni describes two types of leaders: "reward-centered" leaders and "responsibility-centered" leaders.

Reward-centered leaders are looking out for themselves and are driven by pride, ego, and fun. According to Lencioni, they are on the hunt for attention, power, status, money, enjoyment, and entertainment. It's all about them, and while they may sometimes act as if they have integrity, when they do, their motivation is to manipulate. As Tim Irwin describes in his book *Derailed,* this almost always ends up a trainwreck and, unfortunately, these leaders take a lot of people down with them.

Responsibility-centered leaders are driven by a higher purpose. They are willing to make both sacrifices as well as the difficult, challenging decisions. They are focused on serving others and being good stewards of what they are given to manage.

As you can guess, it is the responsibility-centered leaders who have the most impact in the long run. They have the right motivation.

Warren Buffett is one of the richest people in the world and a man known for integrity. I liked what he said as part of a 2018 interview in *Inc.* magazine. Buffet said, "In looking for people to hire, you look for three qualities: integrity, intelligence, and energy. And if you don't have the first, the other two will kill you. You think about it; it's true. If you hire somebody without integrity, you really want them to be dumb and lazy."

Sometimes it can be frustrating to see someone who lacks integrity seem to be rewarded for their poor character. I am convinced that in the long run, integrity pays off not just in business but in peace of mind and better relationships. Even if it doesn't, it is still the right thing to do.

Reflections

- A reputation for integrity is more important than any award.

- Integrity is not only right, it is smart business.

- Motivation matters: "Responsibility-centered" leaders create the best organizations.

PEOPLE

Chapter 6

Eye for Talent

CEOs get too much credit when things go well and too much blame when they go wrong. Our company has had a decade of record results, and while I appreciate receiving affirmation for my part in that, I am under no illusions. We have an amazing team that gets those results, and I am fortunate to be part of it.

To be honest, I have always suffered a little bit of imposter syndrome. I look at our team at Correct Craft where I serve as CEO and see people far smarter and more talented than me. It makes me wonder why I am the leader. I tend to be more of a big-picture thinker, and while I can get into the details if necessary, I am not really wired for them. If we did not have a lot of really smart and really talented people at our company to work with me, it would be a trainwreck.

Hiring smart people and helping them become even smarter may make you feel like the weak link, but it is impossible to have a great organization without great people. This seems like a no-brainer to most people, but many leaders have a hard time hiring people smarter and more talented than themselves. Maybe it is insecurity or fear of losing control, but in organization after organization, their results are limited by the leaders' fear of hiring smart and talented people.

Good leaders need more than just smart people around them. They need people who see things differently. They are open to the perspective of those who have a different view, which makes them better leaders and makes their organizations stronger.

Years ago at Correct Craft, our then-HR Director, Shirley, was a high F on the Myers-Briggs Temperament Instrument (MBTI), while I was a high T—the exact opposite of each other. I will write more about MBTI later in this chapter, but our differences could have led to conflict and, since I was the boss, Shirley likely would have deferred. However, I valued Shirley's temperament and more than once specifically told her I needed her help and wanted her to speak up if she thought I was making a bad decision. I want to have more "F" in my thinking and needed her to help me with that.

As leaders, we will not reach our potential unless we are willing to hire people who are not only smarter than us but also think differently. We just need to accept that.

Patrick Lencioni

As with many other leaders, I am a Lencioni fan. If you talk to me much about leadership, it won't be long before I mention a concept from one of Patrick Lencioni's books. A few years ago, I was surprised on a flight from Orlando to Salt Lake City; while waiting for takeoff and reading one of Lencioni's books, a man sat down next to me and asked what I thought of the book. It was Lencioni himself.

At the time, I was new at my Correct Craft CEO job, and the going was rough. As mentioned earlier, I was the fifth CEO in five years, and I had a mess on my hands. Many members of our team were rightfully skeptical after what they had been through the past few years, and most wondered how long I would last. I was telling Lencioni about the situation, and he drew me an illustration on his Delta napkin. In short, he told me that one-third of our team would enthusiastically follow me, one-third would oppose change, and another one-third would be in the middle waiting to see what happened. Lencioni encouraged me to not focus my attention on trying to convert the one-third who were negative but to invest my energy in the one-third who were on board.

Lencioni's counsel changed my trajectory at Correct Craft and was one of the reasons we were able to move past those difficult days. Even today, I work hard to affirm and invest in those who are on board with our vision, values, and strategic plan.

That doesn't mean we don't encourage debate and conflict. In fact, just the opposite—we promote it. Great teams cannot achieve their best results without struggling with each other's perspectives. However, that conflict cannot take place successfully without a foundation of trust. People who have a high level of trust with each other have an easy time being transparent, which leads to increased effectiveness and great results. Without trust, it is impossible to be effective as a team.

Lencioni best describes this dynamic in his excellent book, *5 Dysfunctions of a Team.* In it, Lencioni explains that trust is the foundation of any team, and a team cannot be functional without it. Once trust is established, a team can have a healthy debate.

At our company, we refer to this kind of debating as "highly assertive, highly cooperative." We expound on this by saying we want no "silent liars." A silent liar is someone who leaves a meeting disagreeing with the direction decided at the meeting but who is unwilling to speak up.

The best leaders want access to the brain power of everyone on their team, and silent lying is not only destructive but also risky for the organization. It results in the group missing important perspectives. Eliminating silent liars requires creating an environment where team members know they can safely speak up; this makes it easier for people on the team who are willing to share their perspective. As leaders, we need to seek those who will commit to not being silent liars.

Finding the Right People

As I have written earlier, when I arrived at Correct Craft in the fall of 2006, it was obvious I needed help. I brought in a friend of mine who had manufacturing expertise to help assess our production processes and another friend with IT experience to ensure our systems were effective and secure. Although they were helpful, I needed more.

In my first meetings with our Correct Craft team, there was a young man, Greg, who really stood out. He said the right things and had great ideas, but he was too far away to help. The young man didn't actually work for Correct Craft—he worked for our Midwest distributor. Finally, to make things just a little more complicated, that distributor was owned by his dad, Ken Meloon, Correct Craft's board chair.

Fortunately, when I approached Ken about Greg coming to help us in Orlando, he could not have been more accommodating. Greg was valuable to Ken in the Midwest, but Ken also knew that if we failed at turning around Correct Craft in Orlando, we wouldn't need a Midwest distributor.

Greg agreed to come to Orlando temporarily to help us with projects that needed to be done, and now, just a decade later, he has become the president of Nautique Boats, Correct Craft's largest subsidiary. Greg is one of the best examples I know of how the right person can make a big impact on an organization.

Greg and I have not always agreed with one another, but that's part of the magic. A team member who sees things differently is valuable, and Greg has insight I don't, so even if I disagree, I ALWAYS listen to Greg, because I respect him and value his opinion.

I initially received criticism about my decision to ask for Greg's help. You would have to understand the dynamic of the time, but Greg was part of the family who had owned Correct Craft for over eighty years, and some people wanted a fresh perspective. I received emails and calls from some of our biggest dealers who questioned my judgment, thinking I had lost my mind by inviting Greg to join us in Orlando. Over the next couple of years, each of those naysayers apologized to me, as they eventually acknowledged the impact of Greg's contributions. Today, no one doubts that Greg is the right person for the job.

Having an eye for talent requires the ability to pick the right person for the job and make tough decisions, even when they are controversial.

With Greg, I got the decision right, but I haven't always made the right decision regarding people. Usually when I make a bad hiring decision, it is because of one flaw in my thinking, which I will share later in this chapter.

Character, Competency, and Chemistry

Many organizations consider their employee-hiring and evaluation decisions within the framework of character, competency, and chemistry. Most don't realize these concepts were originally described by Aristotle as ethos, logos, and pathos. Whether looking at them from an English or Greek view, they are powerful concepts.

Character refers to a person's integrity. This includes their ability to set aside personal interests for the good of a group. People with character base their lives on core principles for which they are willing to sacrifice. Character can be evaluated by examining either how a person has historically reacted in difficult situations or how they act when they have the opportunity to get away with something that would seemingly violate their principles.

Competency refers to a person's ability to do their job. It can be evaluated by education, certification, and experience. Chemistry refers to a person's ability to get along with and work well with others. Some people have natural chemistry, and others are naturally quiet, which can hurt their chemistry. However, the root cause of chemistry issues often connects back to one of two problems: either putting tasks over people or a lack of self-awareness. Often both.

The best teammates have all three characteristics: character, competency, and chemistry.

The consistent hiring mistake I have made throughout my career is to overvalue competency. Of course, I would never knowingly hire someone with bad character or chemistry, but I can be blinded by high competency, which causes me to either overlook character and chemistry or downplay the negatives in these areas. Unfortunately, over the years, this has put me in the position of having to ask some highly competent people to leave our organization after the chemistry and/or competency issues became unbearable.

Focusing on character, chemistry, and competency provides me the best framework to evaluate current and prospective team members.

Temperament Assessments

Shortly after graduating from college and working at the CPA firm, C&L, I was asked to complete a temperament assessment. It was a two-sided form and required me to mark words I believed described me on one side of the form and mark words describing how other people expect me to act on the back of the form. I was curious about the assessment, but other than that, I didn't think much of it.

A couple weeks later, the managing partner of our location, Warren, called me into his office and went over my results. I was fascinated to learn about myself from the results; it really got my attention when Warren said that my assessment scored similarly to his. As a twenty-two-year-old who wanted to be as successful as Warren, that sounded good.

Little did I know that meeting with Warren would begin a career-long fascination with assessments and how they can be used to make both us and our teams better.

Later, after leaving C&L, I would bring another friend of mine, Pat, into companies where I worked to help us with assessments. It was like magic. Pat could read the assessments of those on our team whom he had never met and provide both an excellent review of the employee's temperament and coaching related to how to help that person in their career.

There are many different temperament assessments. C&L used Predictive Index (PI), and I used it for many years at my various companies. Later, I became certified in both Myers-Briggs (MBTI) and DISC, and I still use each of them today. They can all help.

Information is readily available on each of these assessment tools, so I won't share much more, other than to say they have all been incredibly helpful and have made our teams stronger. I have taught both MBTI and DISC to many groups, and they are always amazed at how much there is to learn about themselves and each other in those classes.

After realizing the benefits of assessments, it is not uncommon for one of our team members to ask if their spouse can also take part in the assessment process. Normally, when I look at the assessments of both spouses together and share what they reveal, the couple will say something similar to, "It's like you have been living in our house." Joking aside, that has happened many times.

I encourage all leaders to do their own reviews and draw their own conclusions about the effectiveness of assessments. I can say without qualification that using tools like PI, MBTI, and DISC have made me a better leader.

Finally, I fully understand how little I can do on my own. I accomplish nothing without a great team, and a great team requires great people. A leader must have an eye for talent.

Reflections

- Many leaders have anxiety about hiring people either smarter or more talented than themselves.
- The best leaders hire the best people.

- The best leaders hire people who think differently than they do.

- Character, competency, and chemistry is a great framework within which to evaluate both your team and potential new hires.

- Temperament assessments can be a great tool to develop not only self-awareness but also great teams.

Chapter 7

Energy

It's the Leader's Job to Be the Energizer

Organizations require energy, and the leader must be the primary source. It takes effort to provide energy to your team, but the benefits to the organization are exponential. Unfortunately, it is easy to be a de-energizer.

Some leaders may not like this role or responsibility, but that doesn't change anything. Whether or not we like it, leaders either provide a team with energy or de-energize them. Here are some ways I have found that help provide energy to a team:

- **Keep reminding the team of your "why":** In his outstanding book, *Start with Why*, Simon Sinek explains the importance of an organization knowing its "why." Our "why" at Correct Craft is "Making Life Better," and it drives everything we do; hardly a day goes by without either me or someone else on our team mentioning it. Having a clear "why" describing an organization's higher purpose is very energizing.

- **Have a clear vision and confidence:** Later in this book, I write about the importance of clarity because when a team knows where the leader is taking them, it provides great energy. This is particularly true when the leader expresses confidence in the team's ability to get to the destination.

- **Be an optimist:** No one wants to follow a pessimist. In his excellent book *Learned Optimism*, Martin Seligman writes about the power of optimism and the energy it provides. An optimistic leader can turbocharge an organization.

- **Don't wear your feelings on your sleeve:** When you are irritated, frustrated, just having a bad day, or are in any other way emotionally angsty, keep it to yourself. Most leaders discount the impact their emotions have on their team, but the impact is many multiples more than they realize. I know it is hard. Like most people, leaders want others to understand how they feel, but when a leader transfers negative emotion to their team, it comes at a high cost.

- **Be a high-affirmation leader:** People get tremendous energy by knowing their leader thinks they are doing well and appreciates them. Some leaders believe that affirmation will cause team members to think too highly of themselves and slack off. I think that's absurd. Other leaders just have trouble giving anyone credit, no matter how well-deserved—and that's sad. In my experience, employees appreciate affirmation. It makes them more loyal while providing them a boatload of energy.

(As an aside, but related to being a high-affirmation leader, in her book *Rebel Talent,* Harvard professor Francesca Gino does a great job explaining why leaders should manage to employees' strengths, not weaknesses. If you pick up the book, her writing on this topic starts on page 153.)

You may have a different style than any of the leaders I have written about above, but it is still your job to provide your team energy. Being an energizer has a tremendous return on investment. If you are sincere, the energy you provide your team will drive great results.

Maybe you'd like a few examples of exactly how energy can affect our moods and actions? Don't worry, I've got you covered.

Sports Crowds

Few would call me "passionate" about sports, but I do enjoy paying attention from the periphery. I follow standings during the regular season and occasionally enjoy reading *Sports Illustrated*, but that is about it. Other than a sporadic playoff or finals game, very rarely will I watch sports on television. I know people who spend hours each evening watching sports on TV, but that is not how I want to spend my time. I guess I would rather be reading. Yes, I know, I'm a nerd.

Despite not being a sports fanatic, I have thoroughly enjoyed the unique opportunity of attending many championship games and events, including the World Series, Super Bowl, Pro Bowl, NBA Finals, Stanley Cup Finals, Olympics, World Cup, Kentucky Derby, Masters Tournament, and a college football championship. And they were thrilling—the energy was off the charts.

Other than my daughter's games, the most exciting sports event I have attended was Game Seven of the 1997 World Series. The Florida Marlins were playing the Cleveland Indians in Miami, and the game went into extra innings. How could it get more exciting than Game Seven, extra innings, where every pitch could change sports history? In the bottom of the eleventh inning, the tension was intense. Edgar Renteria was up and hit a walk-off single, allowing Craig Counsel to score from second base and giving the Marlins the World Championship. The stadium erupted. Nearly 70,000 people went from being extremely stressed to jubilant in the matter of seconds. It was a once-in-a-lifetime experience.

The second most exciting sports event was the Belmont Stakes on June 6, 2015. After a thirty-seven-year Triple Crown drought, that week, it looked like American Pharoah had a real chance to earn horse racing's highest honor. Since our family had always enjoyed horses, we made a last-minute New York trip to attend the race and hopefully see history. And history we saw. The tension was palpable, and as American Pharoah went into the homestretch with a lead on his way to victory, there was enough energy at the Belmont to power all of New York City.

Imagine the impact at our organizations if we could capture that kind of energy.

Don't Take That Call

How often does your phone ring or buzz and a name shows up on your caller ID that fills you with dread? Often that is because you know the upcoming conversation is certain to suck you dry of energy. It is interesting how one person or call can have so much negative impact on your energy level.

How does your team react when they see your name on the caller ID or if you are walking toward them in the office? You can be either a huge source of energy for your team or a huge de-energizer; if you choose to be an energizer, it will have a material positive pact on your organization's results.

The ability of leaders to motivate groups is well-documented, but that motivation can be positive or negative. Work to inspire rather than to motivate through fear of repercussions.

Growing up in an evangelical church, we had certain guest pastors who would visit our congregation and energize the crowd. When they were speaking, the crowd wanted to "charge hell with a squirt gun," as we used to say. Those pastors were motivational speakers along the lines of a Tony Robbins or a Zig Ziglar, and they could provide a group tremendous energy. I still attribute a big part of my career-long obsession with wanting to develop myself and others to a motivational speech I heard Zig Ziglar give nearly three decades ago.

You don't have to be a preacher or motivational speaker to create needle-moving energy. Fortunately, there are things all leaders can do.

Presidential Energy

I have been blessed with the opportunity to meet several U.S. presidents, and three of them demonstrated to me their well-earned reputation for being inspirational.

Ronald Reagan spoke at my college, and I arrived very early to get a spot in the front row. I waited a long time with secret service agents and organizers for him to arrive. After his speech, I walked right up to him and shook his hand. President Reagan gave me a wonderful gift as he stopped, shook my hand, looked me in the eye, and for those few seconds seemed to be totally focused on me. It was an amazing feeling. Unfortunately, it was before everyone had a camera with them; I would love to have a picture of that moment. If Ronald Reagan can do that for a college student, certainly we can do that for the people we lead.

Bill Clinton has a reputation for being a high extrovert and making everyone he meets feel like a million bucks. I met him after he was out of office at a private event in Orlando. President Clinton put his arm around me, looked me in the eye, and asked me for my name and what I did for a living. After spending just a couple of minutes with him, it was obvious that he has the ability to energize people, and I am certain that skill is a big part of the reason he made it so far.

Finally, I had an opportunity to meet Barack Obama in the Oval Office, an encounter I will explain and describe in my next book, *Education of a Traveler*. Walking in the Oval Office, I shook the President's hand and said, "Good morning Mr. President, my name is Bill Yeargin." President Obama looked me in the eye and said, "I know who you are, and you build great boats." He went on to say his daughters had been to a summer camp that used our boats and being on them was a highlight of their experience. I realize he had been briefed on me and our meeting, but he did not have to take the time to say his daughters had enjoyed our boats. I could see why he inspires so many people.

It is interesting that none of these presidential encounters were that long, but they were very energizing. Providing energy to a team has a significant positive impact with just a little effort on the leader's part.

Still Working at One Hundred

Ralph Meloon was an exceptional man who lived to be over one hundred years old and regularly came into his office at our company, even in the last couple years of his life. Ralph was the son of Correct Craft's founder, but at the time of his death, he had not owned any stock in our company for a couple of decades. That did not stop him from coming to the office every day and encouraging our team, well into his nineties. Ralph was not a "rah-rah" guy, but he provided our team with tremendous energy. People knew that Ralph had high integrity, cared about them, and wanted them to succeed, and they found that highly energizing. His genuineness was inspiring. We miss Ralph for a bunch of reasons, but one of the things we miss the most is the energy he provided.

Be the Type of Employee You Want to Work With

I have been blessed with a lot of personal energy, so providing energy to an organization may come a little easier to me than some other leaders. However, whether it is easy or not, a leader must find the best way to provide the energy their team requires. As leaders, we want to accomplish extraordinary things. In order to accomplish the extraordinary, a team needs to have a lot of energy—and that needed energy comes from its leaders.

Reflections

- To accomplish extraordinary things, teams need a lot of energy.
- A team's leader can either be an energizer or de-energizer.
- A leader should be intentional about providing their team energy.
- There are things a leader can do to provide their team energy.

Chapter 8

Transform

Transformers don't make things *better*, they make them different.

Articles, blogs, and books are quick to tell people how they can advance their career. They sell people who are hungry to figure out the best way of climbing the corporate ladder the idea that they need to have goals, to network, to develop organizational skills, to take classes, to dress right, to dream big, to have a mentor, and a slew of other suggestions. While they are all good ideas, they won't move you up many rungs of the ladder.

And no, the one thing to do is not related to LinkedIn.

LinkedIn is a great networking platform, and I, like many others, have an account on it. However, while it is possible that LinkedIn may lead to a connection that lands you a job, take a close look at the site. Who differentiates themselves on LinkedIn? Hardly anyone. There are a zillion sharp-looking people on LinkedIn who list all their wonderful accomplishments. Again, not a bad idea, but it's not the key to differentiating yourself and moving up.

Maybe the misguided idea I find the most interesting—one I have seen people incessantly chase—is the premise that to move up the corporate ladder, a climber's resume must demonstrate continual expansion of responsibility. The idea is that future job opportunity is limited by a lack of job title growth. I guess that's not a bad idea, but it's also not one that is going to help you lock down a dream job.

These ideas sell a lot of books and generate plenty of clicks, but I am not convinced they are moving people through the corporate hierarchy.

In order to create as much clarity as I can, everything I have mentioned so far in this chapter is a good idea. All these things will be helpful in your career to help you get raises and to help ensure your job security. They just won't assure you a trip up the corporate ladder.

So, what does?

Good Ideas Are Sometimes Born in Canada

Years ago, just before our family left for a vacation in Western Canada, I was counseling some employees on what it takes to move up the corporate ladder. Employees who show up on time every day, work hard, take part in the company development program, and have good attitudes were wondering why they were not advancing in their careers, or if they were, why it wasn't happening faster.

These employee conversations were on my mind while driving on Canadian Highway #1 from Banff to Lake Louise. Maybe it was time away from my normal routine or the beautiful scenery my family was enjoying, but while driving that mountain highway, I had a breakthrough, an epiphany. Or at least it was one for me.

Suddenly, the answer to these employee frustrations became clear. Of course, I was excited and had to share the idea with my family, which they just love me doing while we are on vacation. Actually, it doesn't excite them, but thankfully, they tolerate me.

My Epiphany

It hit me that *good* employees fall into three categories: maintainers, improvers, and transformers. All three categories include wonderful employees who are needed by every organization, but there is one group that is most likely to move up.

Maintainers are the backbone of an organization. They include people like my father who are incredibly loyal to their teams and show up every day with the desire to work hard and do whatever is necessary for their company's success. My dad was not a corporate ladder-climber, but he was essential to his organization, a contributor who added value for thirty-five years. Dad was an incredible employee, as we learned from his co-workers when he had to go out on disability. But he had other more important priorities than ladder-climbing, such as his family and church, and he was happy to come home to us each day at 4:30 p.m. I am very thankful for that.

Organizations cannot operate without maintainers. They are people who keep the business running. They should be treated well and with respect. Without maintainers, there is no business.

Improvers are also important to an organization; they make things better, and often, they effectively lead teams. Improvers are also imperative because they not only maintain but also help move the organization forward. Often, improvers get frustrated because they know they make things better at their organization but don't understand why they don't make it into the top spots.

Organizations cannot operate without improvers. They work with the maintainers to ensure goals are met and exceeded. Without improvers, there is no business.

Just as the name implies, transformers are the people who significantly change things for the better. They are creative and innovative and, more importantly, ensure their team isn't just doing things right but that the team is doing the right things. In other words, transformers not only make sure the team is using the best techniques and saw to cut down the trees, but they also ensure the team is in the right forest. Transformers don't find a better way to accomplish goals, they find a different way. When transformers share great ideas, others often think about how obvious the idea is and wonder why no one else thought of it, but people often can't see the new way until the transformer points it out.

Let me say it again: Transformers don't just make things better—they make them different. Anyone from these three groups can climb the corporate ladder, but those who generally go to the top are transformers.

Organizations can operate without transformers, but they are likely in a death spiral. Maybe a slow, even imperceptible death spiral, but if an organization is not transforming, they are definitely dying.

The fact that transformers often get the top jobs can be extremely frustrating to maintainers and improvers, especially since they often do not realize what is happening. It can be particularly frustrating if they see areas where they are better or work harder than the transformer.

You might disagree with me as you read this chapter, thinking of a glaring example from your career of a maintainer or improver moving up to the top of an organization. Of course, there are examples of that. It's not that a maintainer or improver cannot move up—it's just that it is way more likely for a transformer to do so.

As I write about later in the innovation chapter, the business landscape is littered with organizations that have offered a great, innovative-for-the-time product but still went out of business. Kodak, Blockbuster, Nokia, Palm, and others are great examples of brands that were part of great companies and run by smart people who were making improvements. However, they did not transform and eventually went away. That is why transformers are so critical and are the most certain to advance in their careers.

For some, this idea of needing to be a transformer to advance seems unfair. They wonder why anyone who is loyal, hardworking, honest, and making the business better shouldn't advance. People with these characteristics do advance and always will. But the surest way to the top is to be a transformer.

So, what does a transformer do? Probably the easiest way to get a list of what transformers do is to flip back to this book's table of contents. Being a transformer is not just doing things right, it is doing the right things.

A Real-Life Transformer

If you look up the word "transformer" in my dictionary, you will see a picture of Paul Singer.

When I invited Paul to breakfast at the Black Bear Diner in Madera, California, most of what I knew about Paul came by way of his outstanding reputation in the boat business. Paul had played a huge part in building one of our industry's largest boat companies, and I was hoping to convince him to become president of our Correct Craft company in Merced, Centurion, and Supreme Boats. At the time, Paul was more interested in starting a ministry at his church, but thankfully for the people he would soon be leading, he chose to see them as his ministry.

Having been involved in some significant business turnarounds, I had no doubt about the challenges Paul was taking on when he agreed to become president of our California company. I knew it would be tough and had high expectations for him; however, I had no idea what a true transformer he was. Paul totally reshaped Centurion and Supreme Boats.

Paul did all the things a new president should do when joining a company that is struggling. He improved margins, reduced expenses as a percentage of sales, built a great sales team that nearly doubled sales, invested in great new product, improved customer service, and developed a marketing program that was impactful and built brand equity. Paul would be the first to say he had an amazing team helping him, but he was leading the group and was creating an environment where all the progress was being made. Doing all of this would be enough to qualify Paul as a transformer, but honestly, it was the least of his accomplishments.

Paul's biggest accomplishment was totally reshaping the culture and team at Centurion and Supreme.

Paul implemented a culture at Centurion and Supreme that dramatically impacted the lives of his team. He was transparent with the team as he gave them information regarding the improvements the company needed. By taking a personal interest in his team members, he developed a culture of care and even started a Bible study for his team. Paul took time to work with them on service projects that improved their community. He set up a reward program for his team that now pays out more each year in employee bonuses than the company used to make in total profit. Paul cared about his team and made their lives significantly better.

Regarding the "nuts and bolts" of the business, Paul kept doing the hard things. In fact, it was part of his constant message to the team. I often heard him say, "We have to do the hard things." Regarding the people, Paul clearly loves and is passionate about his team. He didn't just make Centurion and Supreme better, he made them different.

The Centurion and Supreme story must be one of the biggest transformations in business history—definitely in our industry. I know that sounds like hyperbole, but it is not. Paul may be the clearest transformer I have met, and as Patrick Lencioni describes it, he is the quintessential "responsibility-centered" leader.

One More Thought

As an aside, but related to moving up the corporate ladder, I cannot count how many times someone has told me they would perform at a higher level if I would give them a promotion or a pay raise or both. In other words, they are saying that they will function as an improver or transformer if promoted or paid more. What they don't understand, though I try to explain, is that it doesn't work that way. You don't get promoted by saying what you will do in the future; you get promoted by excelling at what you are doing now.

The best leaders don't just maintain or even improve their organizations; they are transformers.

Reflections

- Leaders are sometimes frustrated when they seem to be doing all the right things but don't advance in the organization as fast as they would like.

- Maintainers and improvers are good employees and critical to the organization.

- Transformers are the ones who normally move to the top jobs.

Chapter 9

Clarity

"Bill, wake up, we have bears on the back porch."

Actually, I have heard those words more than once. We live in Central Florida on the east side of the region in an area known for bears; by some accounts, we have hundreds of them in our county. We occasionally see them in our yard, usually at night, though they have been known to make appearances in our community during the day.

This particular night, the bears were on the back porch, and we were a little concerned that they would come in for a visit, breaking through the glass doors heading out the back of the house. That was not an adventure I wanted, so I grabbed my gun. (Don't hate me, gun control folks, it's just for protection.) I found a nice spot on the staircase from where I could watch the bears. My wife grabbed a foghorn, and the noise from it scared most of the bears away with just one huge bear staying, staring into the house from the porch. I sat and watched the bear and would have sworn its head was turning back and forth, casing out the house. I expected it to come through the glass doors at any moment. I did not want to shoot a bear but definitely would have if it broke into the house.

Of course, my cautious wife counseled me to be very careful and be sure I knew what I was shooting before pulling the trigger, to which I replied, "Anyone or anything breaking through that door tonight is getting shot!"

Okay, I am embarrassed to write this next part, but it's important to my point, so I will. After a bit, we turned on some outdoor lights and realized the huge remaining bear was no bear at all; it was a big chair we had on the back porch. Thankfully we finally turned on the outdoor lights and got some clarity.

Like me that night, our teams need clarity. It is one of the most important things a leader can provide.

Learning at Our New Companies

Our company has done many acquisitions over the years, and one of the first things we do when the deal closes, after the initial integration, is work with the acquired team to prepare a new strategic plan. Developing a good strategic plan requires good baseline information, and one of the ways we get that information is by conducting an employee survey. We have done a lot of these employee surveys over the years, and whether the company is well run or poorly run, every organization's employees want clearer communication.

The consistency we observe in every group of employees wanting more and better communication is probably the most predictable thing we see at companies we acquire. Employees have a deep-seated desire to know what is going on at their company. As leaders, we need to provide good and clear information.

What Should We Communicate?

Communication with your team falls into two categories: information employees need to know and information employees would like to know. As leaders, it is our job to make sure everyone knows what they need to know and do the best we can to ensure people know what they would like to know. It is critical that we provide clarity to our teams.

Leaders need to be crystal clear about what is important to their organization and team. When leaders are unclear, it causes confusion within the organization and creates a lot of wasted effort. Peter Drucker said that there is nothing more wasteful than being good at something you should not be doing. When people are unclear on the direction of the organization, they are likely to be doing things they should not be doing and maybe even getting good at it. As Drucker says, that is a huge waste.

Leaders must clearly communicate the "why" of an organization. Simon Sinek does a great job explaining this in his excellent book *Start with Why*. The "why" at our company is "Making Life Better" for everyone, from our team to the people we help on mission trips. That much is clear to everyone. Every team needs a bigger purpose than just making widgets and money, and creating clarity around the "why" helps create this purpose.

It is also important to keep the big-picture view simple. When I arrived at Correct Craft, the company had a very detailed vision, mission, and purpose. At our first executive team meeting, I had a copy of that vision, mission, and purpose and asked the executives to tell me what it was; no one could. They were great people, and the sentiments were good, but the statements were so complex that no one could have remembered them. I changed them on the spot. If your mission, or your why, is not easy to remember and understand, it needs to be changed.

It is also important to be very clear about performance expectations, which we classify at Correct Craft company into three different types: financial, cultural, and eternal. Each of our organizations have a clear strategic plan that identifies both these expectations and what we need to do to achieve them. We are trying to create clarity.

From Your Head to Their Ear

How often do you hear someone say something that makes no sense? You may wonder, "What did they just say?" or "Where did that come from?" Sometimes this happens because the message is clear in the communicator's head, but when it comes out of their mouth, it is not so obvious to the listener.

Try this. Pick out a relatively well-known song and tap out the song's beat on a table with a friend or co-worker listening. The song can be *Happy Birthday*, *Row Your Boat*, *Jingle Bells,* or any other common song. A high percentage of the time, the song will be clear in your head but remain a mystery to the listener. Sometimes it seems strange to the tapper when they realize the listener cannot name the song; it is so clear in the tapper's head.

This happens all the time with normal communication. Just because something is clear in your head does not mean it is clear to your listener. As leaders, we must ensure that what we are communicating is presented in a way that is crystal clear to the listener.

Improv Improves Communication

One of the most fun activities our family has done is take an improv course at SAK Comedy Club near our home in Central Florida. It was a blast, not only teaching us a lot about ourselves but also getting us out of our comfort zones. I would highly recommend it.

One of the fundamental principles of improv is the concept of "yes, and" which basically means you are always building on the idea of the person who speaks before you. No matter how outrageous a comment is, a skilled improvisator will take that idea and build on it. This same "yes, and" concept can have a significant positive impact if used in our own team's communication.

Nothing stops ideation faster than negativity. As leaders, we need to keep communication going by minimizing the criticality in our discussions. Someone who gets shut down by the boss is not likely to speak up again, which means the leader and organization lose needed brain power.

Ideas to Help Communication

It is hard to be a good leader without being a good communicator. Some ideas that will help with communication are:

- **Be a good listener:** Effective listening helps leaders understand other perspectives, which aids them in presenting their position. One of the most effective ways a leader can get their point across is to carefully listen to and understand other perspectives.

- **Non-verbal communication:** Some experts say that 93 percent of all communication is non-verbal. People will believe how you act way more and faster than they will believe what you say. The most effective communicators, those we say have charisma, have very effective non-verbal skills.

- **Use props:** at Correct Craft, we have created what we call our culture pyramid. It captures our key values on an easy-to-understand graphic. I use this pyramid nearly every day to emphasize what is important to us with people both inside and outside of our organization.

- **Be optimistic and energetic:** The best communicators are optimistic and provide the listener with energy. Making people feel good helps your message. We have all heard it said that "people may not remember what you said, but they will remember how you made them feel."

- **Be concise and direct:** What do you think when you are listening to someone use a hundred words for a message that could be said in ten? Don't be that person.

- **Ask for action:** Have you ever finished a conversation and had no idea what the other person wanted? Don't be that person either. Be clear about what you need and ask for action.

- **When you have made the sale, stop selling:** Once another party has agreed to do what you need or want, stop talking. At that point, you can only add confusion or, worse, give them a reason to change their mind.

Creating and Reinforcing Clarity

There are few things that drive organizational performance more than clarity. As leaders, we take a big step toward helping our organizations optimize performance when we are clear about our "why," our vision, our values, our plans, and our expectations regarding returns.

Patrick Lencioni (yep, him again) writes a lot about being clear and addresses one of my biggest personal challenges with creating clarity. I sometimes feel like a broken record repeating the same things. However, Lencioni encourages leaders to keep repeating their message to create clarity even if they find it boring.

At almost every meeting I have with the leaders or other employees at our companies, I remind everyone of and emphasize our vision—our "why"—and our values. Our leaders know the four pillars to our company vision, we all know our "why," which is "Making Life Better," and we all know our values, which are clearly identified in our company culture pyramid.

It takes effort to create clarity, but the best leaders find a way to do it.

Reflections

- Employees want and need good communication.
- We must communicate what people need to know and try to communicate what they want to know.
- Great leaders believe in and communicate a higher purpose for their teams.
- Keep reinforcing your vision, your "why," and your key values, even when you are tired of repeating them.

Chapter 10

Employee Development

Sam, a leader at our SeaArk plant in southern Arkansas, said, "If four years ago, someone had told me how much I was going to learn here, there is no way I would have believed them."

Our organizations can rise no higher than our people can take them.

"It is better to train people and have them leave than to not train people and have them stay," Zig Ziglar said at a conference I attended in the early 1990s. Those words changed the course of my career.

There are few things I enjoy more than helping someone learn something new. Shortly after getting my master's degree, I began teaching courses as an adjunct professor at our local college and found great satisfaction in helping the students develop. It felt like their lives were changing right before my eyes as they worked hard to improve.

During the 1990s, I started weekly management development classes at Rybovich, which I taught for nearly fifteen years. Our team was energized to both learn together and improve our results because of what we were learning. We were becoming better together.

This was also the time when I started speaking at conferences all over the globe. At conference after conference, people shared what they had learned, and it was exhilarating. Businesses and our industry were improving, and playing even a small part of that improvement was thrilling.

I have been passionate about developing our team at Correct Craft. Though the company was over eighty years old when I arrived, I was Correct Craft's first-ever MBA. However, since then, we have supported about 30 other employees who have gone back to school to earn theirs. Additionally, we have sent employees to all kinds of classes and supported them as they worked to get degrees and certifications. A few years ago, we even developed Correct Craft University to not only encourage our team to learn but to also provide them an easy way to do so. There is no question about it—our team has a passion for learning.

I have been able to see firsthand the benefits to both people and organizations of developing employees and creating a learning organization. It truly is life-changing for the employees and transformative for the organizations.

Improve or Suffer Entropy

If you are like me and cannot remember every detail regarding the Second Law of Thermodynamics, you may have forgotten about entropy. In a nutshell, entropy is quite simple: All systems in our universe tend to become more disordered with time. We deteriorate.

My mind tends to make an association between entropy as a principle of science and entropy in the world of our everyday lives. As leaders, are we and our teams, as well as the systems we create, exempt from this scientific law? No, of course not. If we are not learning, we are falling behind.

Entropy can be a very dangerous—even deadly—force in our businesses. In extreme circumstances, if we are complacent, it will put us out of business.

Any segment or aspect of your business that is not continuously improving runs the risk of deteriorating. Not only do you need to stay focused on managing all aspects of your business, but you must always regularly work at improving them. The less you focus on improving your business, the greater the likelihood that entropy is going to take its toll. And when entropy takes its toll on an organization, it's not pretty.

Training with people from other organizations can be especially helpful at avoiding entropy. Hearing outsiders' perspectives can help both you and your employees break out of negative paradigms, expand your thinking, and learn better ways of doing things. Your employees will also meet others who may help them see your issues from a much broader perspective.

As leaders, we need to have a development mentality. Make employee development important at your organization. Always look for development opportunities. Don't deteriorate; focus on continuous improvement.

Employees Are Loyal When Leaders Invest in Them

There are two primary reasons I hear from leaders for not investing in employee development.

The first is a fear that the employees will leave. The second is cost.

At the beginning of this chapter, I shared a Zig Ziglar quote about not training people that had a huge impact on me. As a reminder, Ziglar said, "It is better to train people and lose them than to not train and have them stay." Many leaders either don't know about or understand this principle and fear their employees leaving after they have invested to make them better. As with most fears, very rarely is this fear realized. In my experience, employees feel a heightened sense of loyalty to employers who are willing to invest in them. The reality is just the opposite of the fear: Employees don't want to leave if we invest in them.

Leaders who think of employee development as a cost are starting out with the wrong paradigm. Employee development is not a cost—it is an investment. Most good leaders today would agree that developing their employees is one of the best investments they can make. Several years ago, I read an article that reported Motorola, the pioneer of Six Sigma, had determined that it gets $33 back for every dollar it invests in employee development. That's a crazy good return, and for most companies, it is the best investment available. When leaders are allocating capital, most will have a tough time beating a 33:1 return!

Build on Strengths

One of the challenges with which leaders wrestle is trying to decide whether to focus on correcting employee weaknesses or building on their strengths. My personal leadership style is more focused on being a high-energy, affirmative leader who builds on strengths, and it has seemed to work well for me. However, I understand it might not work well for every leader.

I also fully understand there are leaders who see this differently than me, and I respect their views. I agree that there often can be glaring weaknesses that are holding an employee back that the leader must address. And, as with any leadership philosophy, there are out-liers that seem to disprove it. People are complicated, and there will always be plenty of examples to disprove any leadership approach.

So, for clarity, before this section of the book is misunderstood, I am not saying that people should not work on weaknesses; of course we should.

However, my experience is that if an employee is operating at a 70 percent performance level, an easier and more certain way to help them increase that percentage is by helping them play to their strengths. Employees may struggle with correcting weakness and pick up a percentage point or two of performance if they manage to do so, but big improvements can be made by helping them play to their strengths.

For example, an employee operating at 70 percent may work dil-igently on a weakness that is hard-wired into them and only increase to performance 72 percent, if at all. That same employee may have an easy path to 85 percent performance by functioning in their strengths.

As leaders, we must work with our team to determine how to achieve the most improvement, but my experience is that often, the biggest gains come by focusing on strengths.

Francesca Gino, an outstanding Harvard professor who I have been honored to study under a few different times, explains this the best in her excellent book, *Rebel Talent*. Starting on page 153 of the book, Gino explains how most organizations have a negativity bias in employee evaluation and development. In some ways, it is the "easy button" (my words, not hers). Gino goes on to document that, "We improve faster in areas where we are strong than in areas where we are weak." I recommend checking out Gino's work for more information on this topic.

Correct Craft University

Over the last fifteen years, we have developed employees in a lot of different ways at Correct Craft. We have brought in outside speakers, had internal speakers, and I have personally taught many leadership development classes. We had a large group of employees go through the Dale Carnegie course, and just last year we had about 30 employees working on their Lean Six Sigma Black Belt through Villanova University.

Plus, we are readers.

Over the years, our team has read dozens of books together, and it is a great way to not only learn together but to also build both comradery and a common language to better develop a learning organization. I know our organization is exponentially better because of our desire to read as a team. In the appendix, you will find books, many of which our team has read together, that have helped both me be a better leader and our team improve.

A few years ago, we decided to better organize our learning under the umbrella of what we now call Correct Craft University (CCU). As part of CCU, we create annual learning plans for our team, and at the end of the year, we recognize those who complete their work. We will usually even throw in a small gift card as a token of our appreciation. Our former HR Director Shirley, who I previously mentioned in this book, travels the country visiting our facilities and encouraging our team to be learners through CCU.

There are a lot of ways to create an employee development program, and I am certain there are many who do it better than us. However, the key is not so much the method leaders use to develop their team as it is the importance of doing something.

Helping Others Become Leaders

As we took off for South Africa on the trip I mentioned earlier in the book, I was sitting next to Wayne Huizenga, and he shared with me how proud he was of the significant opportunities he had given others. He said that true leaders don't create followers, they create other leaders. Those words impacted me, and I wanted to emulate Wayne in that way. Actually, I would like to emulate Wayne in a lot of ways, but this may be the most important: I want to invest in our team.

Some leaders are not willing to invest heavily in their teams. Sometimes it is insecurity, other times a feeling that they are losing control, and often, as mentioned above, it is a concern that if they invest in people, the people will leave. None of that logic—if it is, in fact, even logical—makes sense.

The success or failure of an organization always comes back to the people in the organization. The best leaders know that the most effective way to improve their organization is to develop their people. Employee development is not an expense—it is an investment with a huge return.

Reflections

- An organization's success, or lack thereof, often correlates with the investment leaders make in their people.

- If your organization is not improving, it is deteriorating.

- When leaders invest in their team, it increases the team's loyalty.

- Build on your team's strengths.

- The method of employee development you use is not as important as intentionally working to develop employees.

- Employee development is not an expense; it is an investment with a huge return.

LEADING

Chapter 11

Culture

Whether you know it or not, and whether it is constructive or destructive, every organization has a culture. Not only is that culture extremely powerful, but there may not be anything else that impacts an organization's results more, whether good or bad.

Organizational cultures generally develop one of two ways: The culture is either developed and nurtured by the organization's leaders, or it develops by itself and takes on a life of its own.

There has been a lot written about the importance of organizational culture by people who communicate much better than I do. So, this chapter is going to take a different direction than the chapters so far. Believing we have a very strong culture at Correct Craft that positively impacts our results, I will use this chapter to share a close look at our culture and how we drive it.

I have tried to be intentional about developing our organizational culture since arriving at Correct Craft. Eventually, it became apparent that we were developing an impactful environment at our company, but the components of the culture felt disconnected. Additionally, we had no clear way to communicate it holistically. So, as part of an early strategic plan, we set out to create a graphic that captured the Correct Craft culture. We ended up with what we now call the Correct Craft Culture Pyramid.

It would be impossible for me to overstate the power of this Culture Pyramid; it is our team's North Star. We barely go a day without discussing it in a meeting. Correct Craft uses the Culture Pyramid as part of the recruiting process with new employees and goes over it with them again in new employee orientation. We reinforce it over and over, and the pyramid can be seen on the walls of our Correct Craft companies. This Pyramid has been used by our team thousands of times as a guide to help us make key decisions. We use it to describe our company to outsiders who want to learn about our business or want to partner with us. Our Culture Pyramid is one of the first things I discuss with an entrepreneur who is thinking about selling their business to Correct Craft. It is our lifeblood.

We have experienced over a decade of record-breaking years, in many areas, and this Culture Pyramid played a huge role in our success. However, while the Pyramid is very powerful as a construct or framework to help us crisply capture the essence of our culture, the concepts themselves are what create the magic. So, let's start at the top of the pyramid and work down to examine the concepts that I believe are important to consider when developing an organization's culture.

Mission

Correct Craft was founded in 1925 by W.C. Meloon, who was a man of strong faith. He created the company mission of "Building Boats to the Glory of God." We still maintain that mission today.

Correct Craft is not a church, and there is no religious requirement of any kind to be part of our team. An employee's faith has no impact on their promotability or compensation.

However, it is still important that any organization have a higher purpose, and we are happy to honor the mission set by our founder nearly a century ago.

Why

Every organization also needs a why, and no one does a better job of explaining this than Simon Sinek in his excellent book *Start with Why*. If you haven't read Sinek's book, take a quick break now and order a copy while it is fresh on your mind—it will have a dramatic impact on your organization.

Our company's why is "Making Life Better." We want everyone we contact to be better off for interacting with us. There are several groups to whom we make this commitment.

- **Our customers:** We want to improve the lives of our customers by providing great products, service, and experiences. Most importantly, we want to help them invest in their relationships by spending time on the water with those they care about.

- **Our employees:** We want to provide our team a great work environment, great pay, and great benefits. We also have plans in place to ensure that when our companies have financial success and that we share that success with our team. Finally, we want to give our team opportunities to invest in making life better for others.

- **Our employees' families:** We want to ensure the families of our team know that we are taking good care of their loved ones by providing a safe work environment and culture that helps ensure they come home energized.

- **Our distributors:** We want to provide our distributors great products and support that helps their businesses thrive.

- **Our vendors:** Correct Craft wants to be a great partner with our vendors and to look out for their interests, not just ours. We want to pay on time, for example, or maybe even early. A few years ago, our bank presented us with an analysis that demonstrated we could save a fair bit of money by paying our vendors just a little bit later. We rejected the recommendation immediately; we want to treat our vendors well.

- **Our industry:** Our team spends a lot of time supporting our industry through events and board service. We produce conferences and events like our Culture Summits that even help our competitors, but that is okay—we want to make our industry better as a whole. We know if we can make our industry better, it will have a huge positive impact on a lot of people.

- **Our community:** We want to be good neighbors in our local communities and work hard to make them better by our presence.

- **Our world:** We want to find ways to help people around the world, most of whom we will never meet more than once, through our service and philanthropic work.

- **Our shareholder:** We want to reward our owner's trust in our team through both our trustworthy stewardship of assets and generation of excellent financial, cultural, and eternal returns.

There is a lot of energy created at an organization that truly works at making life better, and the mission creates tremendous energy for our team.

After the why of "Making Life Better," we focus on the three pillars of our culture: **people, performance, and philanthropy**.

Let's focus on those pillars individually. We will start with **people:**

People

Hopefully a clear theme of this book has been the importance of developing and nurturing a great team to achieve an organization's optimal results.

- We want our employees to be well-rounded, so we invest in them **spiritually, physically, and financially.** Weekly Bible studies, weight loss and fitness initiatives, and courses on personal financial management, all of which are optional, are just a few of the ways we have been able to invest in our team.

- We encourage our team to be **highly assertive and highly cooperative**. To be successful, we need our employees to be open and honest and share their different perspectives.

- **Humility** is an important part of our culture. Regardless of how much success our team has, we understand the importance of remaining humble. For those interested in learning more about this, no book demonstrates the damage caused to an organization by a leader's pride better than Tim Irwin's *Derailed*.

- Our version of work hard, play hard is **focused and fun**. We all want to work hard and get a lot done, but there is no reason we cannot do that and also have fun. We want our team to enjoy coming to work.

Performance

With a Mission of **"Building Boats to the Glory of God"** and a why of **"Making Life Better,"** people sometimes think that performance is a secondary priority to our company. That could not be further from the truth. We know that to carry out our mission and our why, we *must* be a high-performing company. There is no inconsistency in caring about people while also requiring our teams to be high-performance. In fact, the latter requires the former.

Our culture pyramid identifies how we try to be high-performance.

- Correct Craft is a **strategic plan-driven** company, and some say our strategic planning process is the key to our success. Each of our companies have their own strategic plan, and those plans powerfully impact results. A good strategic planning process will start with a comprehensive situation analysis that creates a starting point. From that starting point, we create overall and divisional goals. Once the starting point and the goals have been determined, the actual plan can be easily developed.

- Regardless of the amount of success we may have, we still embrace the idea of **continuous improvement.** Remember entropy from a previous chapter? An organization that is not improving is deteriorating.

- **Right and fast** is a concept developed several years ago by one of our team, Sean. Any team can be right with enough time, but the best organizations are both right and fast; that's what keeps them competitive in the marketplace.

- Correct Craft is a **customer-focused** company. We are here to serve our customers with products and services that they enjoy and are proud to own. We understand that great customer products and service requires exceeding expectations.

- Most companies strive to be market-driven, but we strive to be **market-driving**. We want to exceed our customer's expectations and provide them products they cannot yet even imagine.

Philanthropy

Correct Craft wants to make the world better by using our platform to help those who most need it, even those who will never be able to pay us back.

- We want to serve our employees and provide **internal support** and assistance to them when they are going through life's challenges. We look after each other. Employees have come together to raise money for each other's medical needs, contributed vacation time when a teammate needs it, and donated items when someone lost their house to a fire.

- We want to serve our community through **local outreach**. Our teams have donated countless hours to local non-profit organizations. We have built several houses with Habitat for Humanity, given clothes and food to the homeless, and helped worthy charitable organizations spread the word about what they are doing. We love our communities and work hard to make them better.

- We offer **global outreach** to people all around the world. Over the years, I have gone with groups of our employees to places like Cambodia, India, Ethiopia, Kenya, Uganda, and countries all across the Caribbean and Central America to help others. We have helped schools and orphanages, done hurricane repair, fought human trafficking, and participated in a host of other projects. Global outreach is probably the most unique part of our culture, but it has a significant impact on both those we travel to help and our team members who participate.

Our culture pyramid describes how we aspire to conduct ourselves. Correct Craft is far from perfect, and we fail often, but we do have a clear picture of our goals. Though this pyramid works well for us, I am certain there are other, and likely better, ways to capture the essence of an organization's culture. As a leader, don't get weighed down by the construct—intentional action is the best way to drive change, whatever the construct.

Finally, leaders *must* model the culture they want their teams to live out. Your employees will follow how you act much closer than they will listen to what you say. For an organization to be intentional about developing and successfully executing culture, it must be modeled by the leaders.

There's a saying that culture eats strategy for breakfast. Without a good culture, nothing else matters.

Reflections

- Culture has a significant impact on an organization's results.
- All organizations have a culture.
- The best leaders are intentional about creating an effective organizational culture.
- Culture is most effective when modeled by the leader.

Chapter 12

Decision-Making

Me, to my daughters probably a thousand times while they were growing up: "Life is full of choices; make good ones."

When the buck stops with you, that is pressure.

Over the years, I have published hundreds of articles, op-eds, blogs, and columns, some of which are compiled in my earlier book, *Yeargin on Management*. Occasionally, I get a sense that an article will really resonate with readers, and that was true with one particular article I wrote on decision-making. As it turns out, I was correct, and I've had numerous people tell me how helpful it was. So, I am going to borrow liberally from that article in this chapter—but first, let's consider why decision-making is so hard.

Why Is Decision-Making Hard?

When I have the opportunity to promote one of our employees into a company president role, it is always exciting for both me and them. I love giving people opportunity, especially an opportunity as big as a president role, and often, it is a dream opportunity for the person being promoted.

There are a few things I always discuss with the leader before they assume their new role, but at the top of my list is sharing something for which they cannot prepare: the weight of responsibility that comes with being the top leader. When someone moves to the top of an organization's hierarchy, there is often a realization that the responsibility they have previously shared with a boss is now all theirs. Of course, they still report to me as Correct Craft's CEO, but I give our presidents a lot of autonomy; it makes them better leaders if they feel both responsibility and accountability.

Leaders with a conscience realize that their decisions have a big impact on employees, the employees' families, and a host of other people. The weight of that responsibility feels heavy. When you combine it with another common challenge—the fear of being wrong—the sense of responsibility can almost paralyze a leader, and the repercussions are felt by both the leader and their team. Good leaders are willing to get outside their comfort zones and force themselves to make tough decisions even when they don't have all the information they would like.

I also like to remind them that their success is much sweeter when they have made the decisions necessary to achieve it.

Probability and Resulting

Ever notice that some people have a knack for making the right decision? Do you wonder if they are lucky, smart, or intuitive? Or a combination of the three? Ever notice that others seem to consistently make bad decisions? Do you wonder why they cannot catch a break?

I was thinking of these questions as I finished former President Obama's book, *A Promised Land.* In this interesting book, the former president shares his perspective on the 2008 election and the first three years of his presidency. While reading the book, something Obama wrote jumped off the page at me, something most readers may not have noticed. He wrote that as president, he very rarely had simple decisions to make and that he was always dealing in *probabilities*. It was the word "probabilities" that made me think about the process leaders use in decision-making.

As leaders, while we may not be required to make the consequential decisions of a U.S. president, we are still making decisions that will have a big impact on organizations and people. Sometimes those decisions end up being wrong even though they seemed right when we were making them. Often that is because of probabilities.

For instance, even if we make a decision that is the right decision eighty percent of the time, one out of five times, that decision will turn out to be wrong, and the negative impact of being wrong may be significant. We often label someone who gets caught by the twenty percent probability a bad decision-maker when that may be untrue—eighty percent of the time, they would have been a hero.

Sometimes the opposite also happens. A leader may make a bad decision, but the low-probability result occurs, and they are labeled an "expert" or "guru" when they're clearly not. People think the bad decision-maker saw something coming that others didn't when they actually just made a bad decision and got lucky. That's why it's smart to make sure you're not taking too much advice from a "one-hit wonder."

In her excellent book, *Thinking in Bets*, professional poker player Annie Duke deals with this conundrum, which she calls *"resulting."* Resulting is when we determine if a decision was good or bad based solely on the outcome and overlook the process used to make the decision, thereby ignoring probabilities and luck, either good or bad. Many of us much prefer to use resulting because it is simple and, frankly, we often don't care how the decision was made; we just want the right outcome.

Improving Your Decision-Making Process

Fortunately, a good decision is still generally a result of a good decision-making process, and there are some things we can do to improve our ability to make the right choice.

Below are five ways to improve your decision-making process and become a better decision maker:

First, clearly identify what you need to decide. This seems obvious, but frequently, it is the biggest decision-making challenge. Often, our team will frame this as, "What is the problem we are trying to solve?" Creating clarity around what is being decided and what problem is being solved will significantly improve the odds of making a good decision.

Secondly, use broad data. The foundation of a good decision is good information. When speaking at conferences, I have often held up a beach ball to make this point; I explain that whatever slice of the beach ball we are standing on will color our perspective. Good decisions need good information from different perspectives. But often, leaders who don't want to make a decision make the mistake of asking for more and more information, frustrating their team. We should be sure to brainstorm while also being aware of diminishing returns and avoiding paralysis through analysis.

Third, think past the immediate impact. Sometimes when we are deciding something important, it is hard to get out of the moment and immediate concern. We need to consider possible unintended consequences. We also need to consider the worst-case impact of our decision, keeping in mind that a low-probability, huge-negative-impact worst case may want to be avoided while even a high probability, but low impact worst case may be within the leader's risk tolerance.

Fourth, have someone play devil's advocate. The devil's advocate was a position first used in the 1500s by popes of the Catholic church to argue against the canonization of a candidate up for sainthood. The devil's advocate's job was to find reasons not to move forward with the canonization. This process is also important in business decision-making and described well in Edward de Bono's book *Six Thinking Hats*.

Fifth, decide based on principle, not emotion. This is probably the toughest way to improve decision-making because when leaders are making decisions based on emotion, they are usually totally blinded to what is happening. Emotion can make our thinking seem very clear, even though it is extremely clouded. Emotion trumps logic every time.

The best ways for a leader to avoid this is to be self-aware and sur-round themselves with a team who not only sees things differently but also is willing to speak up when the leader is emotionally hijacked.

I suspect there are some leaders reading this chapter thinking it might be good for others, but they have a great track record of making good decisions on their own. I understand that feeling. However, I also know that probabilities will catch up with even the best decision-mak-ers. Using the steps above will help leaders ensure they have a good process even if the outcome is negative.

As I have already written about, one of our key values at Correct Craft is the idea of being both "right and fast." It is easy to be right if you have enough time, but being both right and fast provides a com-petitive advantage. Sometimes even with the best process, you will still be stung by an unlikely probability; however, the above steps will help improve the probability of making good decisions and ensure that your organization is both right and fast.

Palm Beach Inlet: Little Changes, Big Consequences

Often, when speaking about the power of choices, I will share the story of a large ship leaving Palm Beach Inlet near to where I have lived most of my life.

The Palm Beach Inlet area is spectacular. Peanut Island, a fun place to relax and enjoy time with friends and family, is just inside the inlet. Behind Peanut Island is the Port of Palm Beach, a busy port with freighters constantly coming and going. When enjoying Peanut Island and the surrounding water, it is common for one of those big freighters to be leaving the port heading out to sea. Some people don't like the big ships, but I think they are part of Peanut Island's charm.

When the freighters leave the Port of Palm Beach and go past Peanut Island and out the inlet, the captain of the vessel has a decision to make. A slight turn of the ship's wheel to the left, and the freighter ends up in Northern Europe; a slight turn of the ship's wheel to the right, and the freighter ends up in South Africa. One very small decision by the captain makes a significant difference in where the ship ends up. That's the way it works with our decisions. The ultimate impact of small decisions can seem disproportionate to the actual choice being made. Small decisions can have a big impact, and we almost always end up where our choices take us.

Being a leader requires lots of decisions; make good ones.

Reflections

- Decision-making can feel hard.
- Leaders, especially those at the top, feel the weight of their decisions.
- A good result does not mean a good decision process was used.
- There are things we can do to improve our decision-making.
- Being a leader requires lots of decisions; make good ones.

Chapter 13

Future-Focused

"My interest is in the future because I am going to spend the rest of my life there." —Charles Kettering

John Naisbitt's book from the 1980s, *Megatrends,* mesmerized me. I had always been curious about the future, but reading Naisbitt's book, in which he used current trends and data to predict the future, really stoked the embers of my fascination. It set me on the path of being an amateur futurist.

Later, in the 1990s, when I was traveling the globe speaking at conferences, one of my most popular presentations was "What Does the Future Hold? How Today's Global Trends Will Impact You and Your Company." I enjoyed doing the research necessary to make this presentation, and people loved hearing about what the future would bring.

We have seen tremendous change in the last hundred years, but in the next decade, we can expect even more change than we experienced during the past century. These changes will impact all leaders, and they will put many of today's organizations out of business.

"The only thing we know about the future is that it will be different." —Peter Drucker

Singularity University

The dramatic rate of global change became clear to me in the fall of 2017 after spending a week in Silicon Valley attending a course at Singularity University. The course included nearly one hundred CEOs from all over the world with fewer than twenty of those CEOs from the U.S.; it was truly a global mix of leaders. It was also incredibly eye-opening as we heard the world's top experts in various technologies explain how exponential growth in computational power was driving technological change like the world has never before experienced.

We listened as experts shared the changes taking place in artificial intelligence, neuroscience, microbiology, the human microbiome, robotics, quantum computing, virtual and augmented reality, additive manufacturing, energy and electrification, the internet of things, and several other topics. It was a whirlwind week, and I was blown away as I realized not only what was going to happen in the years ahead but also what is actually happening today. As they said during the course, "The future is here today, it is just not evenly distributed."

> **"The future depends on what we do in the present."** —Mahatma Gandhi

Technological Change Will Reset the World

This dramatic change over the next decade will be coming from a lot of different sources, including technology, and it will reset life as we know it.

As leaders, we need to be prepared, or this change will become, without hyperbole, an existential risk for our organizations. We must take our interest in the future beyond mere curiosity and become intentional about focusing on global trends and using what we learn to prepare our current organizations for a different environment.

Some of the technology changes for which leaders should be preparing are:

- Artificial Intelligence (AI) is evolving quickly. Speeding up AI development is cloud computing, which can automatically share what one AI system has learned with others. Vladimir Putin predicted that whichever country leads in AI will rule the world. The day will come when computer power surpasses human thinking.

- Biotech, biometrics, and genomic advancements will soon significantly change both how we live and how long we live. We have seen a sneak peek of this during the pandemic. The entire medical community and how we interact with medical providers will be changing soon.

- What we have learned the past twenty years about our microbiome is also dramatically changing medicine and how we will be treated for ailments. Learnings in this area have the potential to impact lifespans as much as antibiotics did in the last century.

- Many think nanotechnology is just "tiny science," but it is much more. Nanotechnology is the manipulation of atoms and molecules to create new materials and products in a way that will eventually disrupt the entire global supply chain.

- Robotics are also advancing quickly. Eventually, they will help us alleviate labor shortages, significantly improve productivity, and lower the costs of products.

- 3D printing, also known as additive manufacturing, will not only lower the cost of production but also dramatically speed up the time to get both industrial and personal goods to consumers. Combining 3D printing with nanotechnology will be very disruptive.

- The "Internet of Things" (IoT) will not only make the internet even more prevalent but will also provide exponentially more information than we have available to us today. It will also significantly improve efficiency, health, safety, and information flow while lowering costs.

- Energy will change significantly as we phase out the carbon-based products we have been using the past 150 years. This will result in lower costs and a much healthier environment.

- Virtual and augmented reality will change how we shop, learn, work, and have fun.

- Quantum computing is the transition from current binary computers to new quantum bits. Quantum computing will allow the development of computers exponentially more powerful than today's technology. Research in this area will make today's supercomputer look like an abacus.

The development of technologies like those above are already well underway and generating a lot of excitement. They will create tremendous global disruption but will also provide many once-in-a-lifetime opportunities. Some of them are real game changers: Quantum computing, artificial intelligence, and nanotechnology have the potential to reset the geopolitical and economic power structure of the entire world. Further development of any of these three technologies could by itself turn the world as we know it upside down.

There will not only be a major reset of companies and people with influence and wealth but also a potential reset of world powers. Power won't primarily be a result of ships and planes but will rest in the hands of whoever controls these new technologies. This will result in emerging entrepreneurs who will wield major global influence. It will also allow small countries that today have little global influence to emerge as major powers.

After attending Singularity University, I realized that the upcoming changes will be transformative and create a lot of wealth, but they will also be very disruptive to existing organizations, putting many of today's companies out of business. We are at an inflection point, and how we react to these changes today will determine if our organizations continue to thrive and lead in the decades ahead. Leaders should not only stay ahead of these changes but also see them as an opportunity to lead the world in technological development.

Our company needed to do more to prepare for the future, so as a direct result of those six days in Silicon Valley, we started a new company devoted entirely to innovation. In the next chapter, I will share the story of this company.

Peter Diamandis has written a couple of books that explain these future changes far better than me. His books *Abundance* and *The Future Is Faster Than You Think* are both must-reads for current or aspiring leaders.

"The future starts today, not tomorrow." —Pope John Paul II

Globalization and Demographics

Global change will come from a lot of different sources, not just technology. A comprehensive review of all upcoming global changes is beyond the scope of this book, but there are a couple others worth mentioning.

The first is globalization. The world is becoming much smaller and is largely connected. World economies are growing and interdependent.

Globalization includes increasing connectivity that shrink the world into smaller markets. This shrinking, facilitated by the ease of communication and travel, makes it much easier to do business anywhere and everywhere. The global economy is growing at a breathtaking pace, and I have seen this firsthand travelling around the world.

China sells three times as many cars as the U.S., is home to many of the world's largest public companies, and is doing a great job of establishing relationships around the globe that will allow it to control the world's most precious resources. The world's tallest building is in the Middle East, Macau is a bigger gambling destination than Las Vegas, India has the world's largest movie industry and refinery, and ninety-five percent of the world's consumers live outside the U.S.

When visiting their countries, I have often been asked by foreign government officials what they can do to attract one of our companies to their country. Leaders around the world have embraced capitalism as the only proven wealth builder for the masses and are competing hard to develop their own economies. There is no turning back.

The good news is that globalization and capitalism are pulling billions of people out of poverty, and those people want more products. The even better news is that this global growth is not reducing any country's specific piece of the pie; global wealth is growing significantly, and globalization is making the overall pie *much* bigger, which benefits everyone.

Many in the U.S. do not like the thought of globalization since we have largely dominated the world stage for decades, but it does not matter what we think—the U.S. has only five percent of the world's citizens, and globalization is already happening—and it is irreversible.

We will all become more dependent on international suppliers and customers. Americans will need to be prepared for more global competition, regardless of the nature or size of our business. Instead of fighting globalization, leaders must well position their organizations for its inevitability. It does not matter if we consider globalization good or bad—it is changing our world in a big way regardless.

Demographics will also have a big impact on our world, and leaders should now be preparing to adapt. There has been much written about demographics, but it just comes down to math.

In the U.S., differing birth rates will impact the look of our country as the Latin population continues to work its way toward eventually becoming a majority in the U.S. Millennials, whose different views on work and life have been well-documented, are close to being a majority of the U.S. workforce and will soon be working their way into political and business leadership.

Globally, the population is growing for now, and the age mix is changing. Fertility rates around the world have dropped, as happens every time a country's wealth increases, particularly in industrialized countries. Lifespans are increasing because of global wealth increases and the impressive improvement in global medical care. Almost all industrialized countries, except the United States, are projecting sizable population decreases in the decades ahead.

People are moving from rural to urban environments, often in coastal areas. This has the potential to be good for those of us in the boat business but is almost certain to hurt others.

None of this is starry-eyed thinking—it is all happening today, and we are heading toward a tipping point that will impact everyone. While potentially bringing significant benefits on a macro level, technology, globalization, and demographic changes will also bring substantial uncertainty and disruption on a micro level. Change is happening much faster than the world has ever seen, and it will materially impact peoples' lives. However, instead of resisting change and doubling down on the past, we need to look for ways to benefit from the inevitable changes to come.

Trying to hold onto the past (like the videotape rental stores over a decade ago trying to keep their customers) just delays the inevitable and extends the agony. However, despite the obvious signs, many people will try to stay in the past. Even most of those who see the changes coming will not know what to do, while those who are smart and forward-thinking will topple today's leaders (both people and companies). *We need to embrace the inevitable and look for ways to take advantage of future changes instead of looking for ways to protect the past.*

We need a bold vision for our organizations that inspires us and our teams to look forward and lead during significant global change. As John Kennedy did decades ago with his call to put a man on the moon, as leaders, we need to inspire our organizations to look forward. We need to inspire our teams to be the clear leaders in both adapting to and creating the future. The best leaders are always looking to the horizon to ensure their organizations are creating disruptions, not becoming victims of them. For leaders who embrace the changes and find ways to benefit from them, the coming years are an incredible opportunity to positively impact their organizations.

In this chapter, we have considered some examples of upcoming changes, but there is much more than what I have shared here. As leaders, we need to be looking ahead for any change that might impact our organizations or provide us with opportunities.

Finally, I know from experience that making predictions is tough. As we discussed in the decision-making chapter, we are always dealing with probabilities, and sometimes the unexpected will happen. However, more important than making specific predictions is a future mindset that is always scanning the horizon for both opportunities and potential existential threat. The best leaders will need to do that in the years ahead.

"It always seems impossible until it is done." —Nelson Mandela

Reflections

- The world is changing dramatically.
- Technology, globalization, and demographics are examples of three areas where change will have a significant impact around the world.
- The impact of the changes will be very disruptive for organizations that cannot adapt.
- The best leaders must continually be scanning the horizon for changes that will impact their organizations.
- The future will provide tremendous benefits to those who view the upcoming changes as opportunities.

Chapter 14

Innovate

Arriving at Correct Craft near the end of 2006, I knew the company had a history of innovation; however, those days had passed, and the company was struggling. With five CEOs in five years, not much attention had been given to innovation. Our team had lots to do but also understood the importance of innovation and that we needed to rekindle our company's rich heritage of excelling at it. So, we got to work.

Before long, we had won an award for having the most innovative product in the watersports industry. This win was huge for our team, and though we have won numerous awards since then, including several for innovation, that first innovation award might still be my favorite. It provided us with the catalyst and momentum we would build on to reach new highs in the following years. Now, in an industry with 35,000 companies, we are recognized as the marine industry's most innovative company. Our company has enjoyed a transformation driven by innovation and executed by a dedicated and talented team. And that innovation set us on a decade of record-breaking results; pushing boundaries has helped transform our company.

Remember, without a great product, nothing else matters. And if your company is not driving innovation, get your resume polished up— you will be needing a new job sooner rather than later. Companies that are not innovative cannot survive in the long run: They are going out of business.

Despite its importance, innovation is a mystery to many leaders. To some, it is all about technology, while others want to innovate but are not sure how to get started.

Then there is the biggest challenge of innovation: It disrupts the status quo, and only very courageous leaders are willing to disrupt their own organization. A leader must sometimes put their organization's current success at risk to prepare for the future, and history teaches us that most leaders find that impossible to do.

The late Harvard professor Clayton Christensen, in his wonderful book *The Innovator's Dilemma,* explains innovation and why organizations fail at it better than anyone. After spending a week at Harvard with Christensen and other innovation-focused professors, it was clear to me just how blinded leaders can be to both the problems noted above as well as to innovative opportunities.

Fortunately, these problems are easily overcome.

It seems simple and obvious to say we should always be innovating, but many leaders don't truly embrace that mindset but instead are fixed in their thinking and the way they do things. Though it is cliché, and they would likely never say it aloud, they think, "If it's not broke, don't fix it." The problem is that these leaders often don't realize that it is broke until it's too late to repair.

Fear of Self-Disruption

The business landscape is littered with examples of leaders who let concerns about disrupting their own organizations keep them from taking the obvious steps needed to survive. Kodak, Blockbuster, Blackberry, Nokia, Borders, and just about every retailer falls into a group of businesses who failed to act. Even when they knew it was necessary, they did not want to disrupt their own business model. Sadly, they all ended up as victims of disruption.

It is interesting that almost every company that has been disrupted out of business had smart managers who considered themselves innovative. Unfortunately for them, they focused on the wrong type of innovation.

Innovation falls into two broad categories: sustaining and disruptive. Many companies are good at sustaining innovation, which makes current products better. Because those companies are good at maintaining that type of innovation, they often consider themselves "innovators"—but that is a big, dangerous trap that sets them on a path to going out of business.

The second type of innovation, disruptive, is named appropriately. Disruptive innovation transforms markets and how customers have their needs met. Companies that practice sustaining innovation make it tougher on their competitors, but disruptive innovators put their competitors out of business. That's a big difference.

Even leaders who understand the different types of innovation often do not realize that it is almost impossible for organizations to be both sustaining innovators and disruptive innovators. Disruptive innovation often requires that organizations put their entire business model at risk; it becomes an existential problem, literally. Sustaining innovators are rarely willing to take the risk of disrupting their entire business. That is why disruptive innovation almost always comes from the outside, even though sustaining innovators may have the same ideas and better resources.

A great example of this is Kodak, a company that invented the digital technology that later put them out of business. Their team was so consumed with their then-current industry leading technology and sustaining innovation that even when they considered marketing digital technology, it was through the lens of their print business. Kodak invented a transformative innovation but could not see it because they were stuck focusing on their sustaining innovation. This mistake cost many Kodak employees their jobs and Kodak investors billions of dollars.

By the way, Kodak's leaders were not stupid. They were smart business leaders who were blinded by their focus on sustaining innovation. Beware—if it can happen to them, it can happen to anyone.

From Idea to Innovation

Ever had a great idea that went nowhere?

Leaders often struggle to develop good ideas into significant innovation. History provides us many examples of great ideas that initially had very little impact.

Over 1,500 years ago, the Roman Empire moved its capital east to Constantinople, and Europe was ushered into the Dark Ages, a period when most people on the continent were in survival mode. During this period of European stagnation, the Chinese began using geared machinery. However, it was not until much later during the industrial revolution in the West that the idea of geared machinery was "discovered," resulting in the creation of significant wealth.

At the same time, Europe was in the Dark Ages, much of the Middle East was not only thriving but was also creative, even producing the first steam engines, another discovery not utilized by the West for centuries. Those are just two of many ideas that needed the right environment to reach their full potential. Both were amazing ideas, but neither was applied by its original discoverer in a way that generated significant economic benefit.

Innovation eventually brought Europe out of the Dark Ages by allowing farmers to produce a little more than their family needed, resulting in excess produce they could barter for needed items. This bartering resulted in new exchange markets at crossroads that turned into cities. Ultimately, wealth-creating innovation combined with individualism, a byproduct of the Protestant Reformation, led to the Renaissance, the Scientific Revolution, a lot of new wealth, and the Western world as we know it today.

Sometimes we get confused about exactly how innovation happens. We are often blinded by "resulting," which occurs when hindsight bias causes us to think someone is an innovator when really, they were just lucky. The danger in this is that we look at their lucky process and give it credibility when it either may be of no value at all or could even inhibit the innovation of others who try to duplicate it.

Innovation can happen through luck or intention. Since we cannot count on being lucky, we need to be intentional about innovation. Plus, being intentional is a great way to also improve our luck!

So, how does a leader who wants their organization to be intentionally innovative get started?

To start with, they create the right mindset. Read the book *Mindset*, written by Carol Dweck and referenced in earlier chapters, with your team. Dr. Dweck explains not only how people get stuck in their thinking but also the ways that it limits a person's potential. She also explains how we can overcome these challenges with a growth mindset, without which, it is nearly impossible to be intentionally innovative.

After you and your team are done reading *Mindset*, read *The Innovator's Dilemma* by Clayton Christensen. It may be the best book ever written on innovation. In short, the *Innovator's Dilemma* states that it is almost impossible for organizations like Kodak, Blockbuster, Nokia, Blackberry to make changes that will disrupt their current business model. However, someone is going to disrupt your model, so it might as well be yourself.

Many leaders think innovation is synonymous with technology, but it is much broader than that—innovation should impact everything we do. It is an outlook that should impact every part of an organization. However, that broader outlook does not diminish the impact of technological change. Increasing computational power is driving change so fast that we will experience more technological transformation in the next ten years than we have ever before seen.

Leaders no longer have time to recognize change along the way and adjust; both technological and non-technological change is coming so quickly we need to expect it and to always be innovating. We need to continually encourage our teams to look for new and creative ways of doing everything, and sometimes, those new ways will include technology, but not always.

Consider how to separate sustaining and disruptive innovation within your organization. At the very least, ensure your team has a high awareness of the innovator's dilemma so they can be on the lookout for it.

Great leaders create tremendous clarity around the importance of innovation to their organization. Make sure everyone knows that transforming products and processes is important to not only the organization's future success but also its survival.

Create the right environment. As leaders, we need to invest, allow failure, and celebrate innovation. That seems obvious, but a surprising number of organizations discourage innovation by having a culture that rewards, extrinsically or intrinsically, those who keep things steady. Only a few would admit it, but many organizations have an "if it's not broke, don't fix it" mentality which creates a culture that frowns on innovation. We cannot get better results if we limit ourselves to doing things the same way we always have done them.

Stop swirling. At our company, it's called "swirling" when we keep talking around an issue without acting on it. The swirling may be about what we should do, how we should do it, or why it cannot be done, but it includes a lot more talk than action. Successful innovators stop swirling, move toward a problem or opportunity, and act.

Make sure you are fulfilling a need. Be sure that what you think is innovation is actually fulfilling a need, even if the need is not at first obvious to the potential customers. Sometimes this is phrased as "What is the job to be done?" or, "What is the problem we are trying to solve?" No matter how innovative you think it is, don't expect to monetize an idea for which people are not willing to pay.

Also, be willing to fail. No one wants to do foolish things; however, having a high risk aversion makes it almost impossible to be disruptively innovative. Backcasting, the process of imagining you have obtained a desired innovative outcome and then thinking back toward how you would have gotten it done, can help. An example of this most of us can relate to is if our goal is to lose twenty pounds, we imagine that the pounds have been lost. Then, we look back and think of what we did to lose the weight. Backcasting can change our perspective on a challenge and make it easier to create an innovative solution.

Innovation is not mysterious—there are proven ways to help your company become an intentional innovator. By implementing the above, it will take you and your organization a long way toward being innovative and maybe even ensure your company's survival.

Watershed Innovation

After attending the course at Singularity University, I was inspired to start a separate entity to focus solely on disruptive technology. At first, I wasn't exactly sure what this new entity would do, but I knew if our company was going to survive the upcoming global changes, we needed to focus on disruptive innovation. So, we created Watershed Innovation.

Watershed Innovation was born with the purpose of identifying, researching, and developing plans to implement disruptive innovation throughout our organization. Our Watershed Innovation team, led by its president, Sean, works on research involving electrification, IoT, robotics, additive manufacturing, virtual and augmented reality, and other opportunities in a way that does not threaten the existence of our other companies.

So far, the results have been phenomenal. As of this writing, we have started a telematics company called Osmosis from scratch, acquired a milling company, started a tooling division, and have researched important topics for our companies such as additive man-ufacturing and robotics.

However, Watershed Innovation's most exciting progress has been made in electrification, with the development of Ingenity, a new company that is building the world's most advanced electric rec-reational boat. We have been selling these boats around the world and are leading our industry in a critical new segment. By creating Watershed Innovation, our company has been able to make exciting leaps in innovation.

As an aside, but I'll mention it again because I am proud of our team, Watershed Innovation has also played an important role in our organization being recognized as the marine industry's most innova-tive company two years in a row. With 35,000 companies in our indus-try, being number one two years in a row isn't bad. We love innovation.

In the previous chapter, we looked at the importance of being future-focused. The logical next step after identifying global trends is to focus on monetizing them through innovation. Smart leaders do just that.

Reflections

-   Companies that are not innovating won't survive.
-   Innovation is not a mystery; a leader can be intentionally innovative.
-   Innovation is more than technology; it is developing new and creative ways to do everything.
-   There are two types of innovation: sustaining and disruptive.
-   Disruptive innovation is best done in a separate entity.

WRAP-UP

Chapter 15

Nuts and Bolts

It was never my intention to write a book about how to run a company, and so far, the thoughts I've shared have been about leadership at a relatively high level. Without diving too deep, in this chapter, I want to touch on some operational ideas that have been important to our team as we have led our businesses. This is a short chapter that will present some high-level ideas on several business areas, but it will not be a deep dive. Hopefully, the thoughts in this chapter will be a catalyst that impacts your thinking and encourages you to do their own research on each topic.

Product Development

The deeper I get into my career, the more I realize that most businesses rise and fall on their product development. Of course, this can also apply to the development of services.

The product development function not only creates the product or service offered to customers, but it also highly impacts the organization's pricing, margins, production efficiency, and quality. If a leader gets those items right, it is almost certain that they will have a profitable business.

Many companies spend a lot of time and money on market research before making product development decisions, and there is some benefit to that—we do some of that ourselves. However, market research is notoriously unreliable. At our companies, we don't want to be market-driven, we want to be market-driving. There is a big difference.

Finally, every leader involved in any type of product development should be familiar with DFMA. DFMA, Design for Manufacture and

Assembly, ensures that the product development team stays focused on developing products and services that are not only exceptional but can also be delivered profitably to a customer. Many organizations, in an effort to improve production efficiency, focus on improving production processes. That seems to make sense, but often, it does not address the root cause of the problem, which is in product development. DFMA helps organizations generate and optimize profitability, but get it wrong, and you're going out of business.

Sales

Selling on price is lazy, and it hurts most organizations. In fact, if a sales team is trying to sell on price, their organization is often in trouble—very few companies can thrive by competing on price. Sales teams must believe their product or service provides value to the customer and sell that value. If an organization has a great product, they should embrace being the most expensive.

Often, sales reps will pull out the concept of price elasticity from Economics 101 to argue that prices should be lower. This is very dangerous because in most cases, the number of incremental units that must be sold just to get back to even is undoable. Furthermore, those same sales reps tend to forget about the concept of price inelasticity taught in the same Economics 101 class (look it up).

And speaking of price, while it is the most efficient way to increase a firm's profitability, it is also probably the most mismanaged part of businesses. Most businesses price based on a cost markup or what their competitors are doing. These are good data points, but they should not be the sole basis for pricing. There are a lot of good resources on this subject that will help you better manage your pricing, including the excellent books *Confessions of a Pricing Man* by Hermann Simon and *Pricing with Confidence* by Reed Holden and Mark Burton.

In a nutshell, sell the value provided to the customer, not price.

Marketing

Marketing is not about running ads or posting on social media—it is about building brand equity through stories.

When I lived in South Florida, Jimmy Buffet was a customer of Rybovich, the company where I worked. He would spend a lot of time hanging out at our boatyard, and most people had no idea he was there. I had the opportunity to go to lunch with Jimmy a few times and was a partner with him in a venture to build boats themed after his work.

Jimmy is an outstanding artist, but he is an even better marketer. He has created an incredible story that built brand equity he can license out for tremendous royalties.

Our company, Correct Craft, and many of our brands also have incredible brand equity because there are wonderful stories that make up their history. People love stories and want to share them. That builds brand equity which, in turn, helps sell more product.

Marketing is building brand equity through stories.

Strategic Planning

At Correct Craft, our team has been able to dramatically grow our company and improve everything we do—literally. Strategic planning has been our secret weapon.

We have a proprietary strategic planning process that produces a clear picture of a business's current position, sets high goals for the next three to five years, and develops a plan to move from the current position to achieve those goals. It is very impactful.

A good strategic planning process can directly improve your business in a big way.

Finance

I have been in three situations, including at Correct Craft, where I joined an organization and quickly realized that the company was operating with incorrect financial information. At Rybovich, I had the accounting team review the cash reports my first day there and found out they were totally wrong. In short, the cash being reported was not there—a really bad way to start.

Not long ago, our team was looking at a potential acquisition and reviewed the company's financial statements. They were a mess. The company was not making money, and the financials were wrong; they were not useful at all to run a business. In fact, we quickly determined they were selling some products at less than cost. Bad financial information was driving that company out of business, and the owner fired this CFO shortly after I shared our discoveries.

I cannot overstate the importance of having a good financial manager in an organization.

One more thought about an important financial concept that many leaders ignore: capital allocation. I read that Warren Buffet's partner, Charlie Munger, said once that the key to their success was nothing magical. It was obtaining capital at three percent and investing it to earn 13 percent. Anyone who can do that will become very rich.

Leaders need to be very careful with how they allocate their capital. First, make sure you are investing it to receive a higher return than the cost of the capital. Second, ensure that the capital is being invested in the optimal way.

The best leaders understand the need for good financial information and strive to optimize the capital they have available to invest.

Production

The best tip I can give related to production or manufacturing is Lean Six Sigma, the body of knowledge that combines the Lean and Six Sigma theories. While I am definitely not a production expert, I did invest the time necessary to earn my Lean Six Sigma black belt and fully appreciate the benefits. Lean Six Sigma can transform a business.

Lean was developed by Toyota in the 1950s, and over the next couple of decades, it transformed the company. Product that was once considered sub-par evolved into today's Toyota and Lexus. Lean focuses heavily on removing waste from processes and improving production flow. Many companies have used Lean to improve their results.

Six Sigma was developed in the 1980s at Motorola and is a statistically driven way to improve operations. The best part of Six Sigma is the DMAIC framework that can be used by any organization, with or without the statistics.

Leaders should ensure those running their production have a good handle on Lean Six Sigma. If your production team does not understand Lean Six Sigma, there is a very high probability your firm is operating in a sub-optimal manner.

Margin Management

Many companies are made or broken on margin management, and unfortunately, few leaders really understand how to manage it.

We use a financial "bridge" to review our margins versus expectations each month. This bridge highlights all the things that have impacted the margin during the past reporting period. Even if you meet or exceed margin in a month, it is important to review margin in detail. An improved margin could be netting out a problem that needs attention but is hidden by something else that is going well.

We have a proprietary method of improving margin that is beyond the scope of this book but focuses on product development, pricing, product packaging, and production. Leaders should review each of these areas to improve their company's margins.

Bad margin management can put a company out of business, and good leaders fully understand the many elements of their organization's margins.

This short chapter could have been a book by itself. Who knows? Maybe my next book will be called *Nuts and Bolts* and cover these topics and others like them in detail. In the meantime, the coverage of the topics in this short chapter is intentionally not comprehensive; however, I hope it will serve as a catalyst to encourage leaders to be learners in each of these areas.

Reflections

- Many businesses rise and fall on their product development.
- Sell the value, not price, provided to the customer.
- Marketing is building brand equity through stories.
- A good strategic planning process can directly improve your business in a big way.
- Make sure you are getting good financial information, and stay focused on optimizing capital allocation.
- Use Lean Six Sigma in production.
- Bad margin management will put a company out of business.

Chapter 16

Musings of a CEO

Remember the Allman Brothers song "Ramblin' Man?" Well, that's what I am going to do in this chapter: ramble. Some topics just don't fit elsewhere in the book but are still thoughts worthy of sharing. Below is a rapid-fire version of them.

Harvard

As a CPA, I needed twenty hours a year of classes to keep my license active. That requirement helped me create a great habit that, even though I transitioned my license to inactive status years ago, keeps me learning. Over the years, I have taken thousands of hours of classes, and I have been blessed to attend classes at some of the best universities in the U.S., including Harvard, MIT, Stanford, and Wharton.

My favorite classes have been at Harvard, where I learned ideas that directly impacted our businesses. In an international business course, I learned the importance of having good local partners when expanding globally and the advantage of being the first mover to serve international markets. An innovation course there helped me understand the difference between sustaining and disruptive innovation and the importance of developing disruptive innovation outside of entities focused on sustaining innovation. In a behavioral economics course, I learned that while most of us think we make rational choices, evidence indicates that almost no one does. Understanding behavioral economics helps us "nudge" people toward the right decisions. Finally, in a negotiation course, I was able to develop a negotiation framework that will make anyone a better negotiator. Harvard courses have had a big impact on my leadership.

Taking courses at the top schools is expensive but also a great investment that can return millions of dollars to your organization.

Timing and Moments

Much of what we accomplish in business is connected to timing and creating the right moments. As I now look back over a career of momentous events, I understand that better than ever. I think most leaders eventually come to the same realization but are too late to really use the idea to lead.

In hindsight, I see how I have benefited from incredibly good timing. Some people would likely call it luck. However, leaders don't have to count on luck because an awareness of timing can help them be much more effective.

Additionally, any time we can create "money can't buy" moments for people, it is impactful. Maybe it is an unexpected call or email to them or an invitation to do something they might not otherwise have access to; sometimes, little things go a long way.

Young leaders don't need to wait until they learn from experience how powerful the moments and timing concepts are. Two great books that will help any leader understand timing and the impact of moments are *When* by Daniel Pink and *The Power of Moments* by Dan and Chip Heath. Both are worth the time to read.

Creativity

Many people would like to be creative but don't think of themselves as creative people—they think it just doesn't come naturally to them. That thinking is a myth and causes many people to lose out on a lifetime of creativity and possibly even robs them of the opportunity to become innovators.

I am going to bust the creativity myth, so please read this paragraph carefully—very carefully. In fact, read it three times before moving on; this paragraph could change your life. Everything I have experienced, read, and observed about creativity indicates that a person's creativity directly correlates with their creative identity. In other words, if you think of yourself as creative, you are; if you think of yourself as not being creative, then you are not.

My wife Leigh is an elementary art teacher, and we believe that what a child is told about their creativity at a young age becomes the self-perception they carry their entire life. By telling a child they are creative, you dramatically improve the odds that they will be. (As I was proofreading this chapter, my wife showed me a card she just received from a student that said, "thank you for liking my art.")

But what about those who did not have their creativity affirmed as a child? The great news is that you can immediately begin thinking of yourself as creative, and it will have instant results. If you begin to think of yourself as creative, you can change your self-identity quickly, which will help you become even *more* creative. This sounds crazy, but I have seen it work.

Leaders who do not think of themselves as creative should commit a month to telling themselves daily that they are. Start working to think of yourself as creative, and I guarantee you will see results. And it always helps to have someone affirm you, so I am telling you right now that I think you are creative because I believe you are. I can't wait until you believe it too and enjoy the benefits of being a creative person.

Necessary Endings

I hate firing people and often lose sleep over it. However, leaders unwilling to make changes when it's appropriate put their entire organization at risk. Sometimes leaders *must* make changes that affect people, no matter how painful it is to us and them.

No one explains this better than Henry Cloud in his thoughtful book *Necessary Endings*.

Interestingly, there have been many occasions when I made a change, and the person impacted contacted me later expressing thanks. I know it sounds strange, but it is absolutely true. Often when a change is needed, the person impacted is unhappy too, and the leader's decision liberates them to move forward and find something more suitable to them.

This Time, It Is Different

Mark Twain once said, "History does not repeat itself, but it rhymes."

One of the things you learn when studying behavioral economics is that people will believe almost anything. One of the things people often believe frequently to support another false assumption is that "this time, it is different."

It happens often, especially, it seems, when things are going well; people are likely to say, "this time, it is different." Generally, the phrase is used when claiming that the normal business cycle or some other fundamental economic principle does not apply to the current situation. When you hear people start talking like that, watch out—there is often trouble brewing.

The book *This Time Is Different: Eight Centuries of Financial Folly* by Reinhart and Rogoff, explains how we all get caught up in this feeling and shares numerous examples of people mistakenly thinking the lessons of history did not apply to them. It is worth the read.

Teamwork

When asked for advice regarding team-building, my go-to recommendation is always a book I mentioned earlier, *5 Dysfunctions of a Team* by Patrick Lencioni. Many leaders aspire to develop strong teams, and Lencioni's book is the perfect starting point.

Teamwork is complex. What some leaders don't realize is that an exceptionally talented employee, the kind we all want, can be bad for teamwork and can sometimes even hurt team performance. The book *Boys in the Boat* by Daniel Brown helped me understand this concept. The book tells the fascinating and real story of nine American men who formed a rowing team that—spoiler alert—won the gold medal in the 1936 Berlin Olympics, disappointing Adolph Hitler and the vaunted German rowing team.

One of the lessons from *Boys in the Boat* is that teams must work in sync to get the best results. If one rower is better than the others but cannot fit into the team, the exceptional rower actually hurts the team. The idea of a talented employee hurting results seems counter-intuitive, but it is true.

Black Swans

As I write this book, the world continues to struggle with COVID-19. It seemed to come out of nowhere, something Nassim Taleb calls a Black Swan in his book aptly titled *Black Swan*.

While it may have been tough to predict a pandemic, we all should have known something was coming. The past one hundred years, we have experienced one Black Swan after another. We had WWI, the Spanish Flu, and Prohibition, which resulted in a crime wave. There was a stock market crash in 1929 followed by the Dust Bowl and the Great Depression. It took WWII to pull the U.S. out of the Depression followed by the Korean and Vietnam Wars. The world had flu pandemics of 1958 and 1968, both killing over a million people. The 1970s brought an oil embargo, high inflation, low economic growth, and interest rates near twenty percent. The U.S. had another stock market crash in 1987, followed by the first Gulf War, Y2K, 9/11 and the Afghanistan and Iraqi Wars. Finally, the Great Recession and now a pandemic. The pandemic may be the latest Black Swan, but the chain of events will not break; we will continue to have more Black Swans on a regular basis.

While the chance of any specific low-probability event occurring may be low, the chance of some low-probability event happening is high.

As leaders, we may not be able to predict what the next Black Swan will be, but we can be sure one is coming and be prepared. Every leader should have a downturn plan ready to execute when needed. That is not being pessimistic, it is being smart.

Results > Activity

Our company has made many corporate acquisitions over the years, and as part of the due diligence process, I meet with executives of the company we might acquire. One thing is highly predictable about those meetings: The executives almost always go out of their way to tell me how busy they are. I have sat in more than one of those meetings wondering why the executive was having such a hard time getting their job done—probably not the impression they were trying to make on their potential new boss.

Many people seem to think that busyness means effectiveness, but that is not true. Leaders should not evaluate themselves or their teams on how busy they are. Often, busyness is not a good sign but rather a sign of ineffectiveness.

As I mentioned earlier, I would much rather a leader work 30 hours a week and get great results than work 70 hours with lesser impact. Unfortunately, we often admire the person who comes in early and leaves late, creating a busyness that takes focus off results.

At our company, many of us have reminders on our desks that say "Results > Activity."

Self-care

While I am clearly not a muscle man, I do thoroughly enjoy exercising. It is so much fun that a few years ago, I went to a university in south-west Florida for three days to become a certified personal trainer, not for work or money but for enjoyment.

I try to exercise in some manner every day, though it gets tough when I am traveling. Clearly, I would not have wished for a pandemic, but a positive effect of COVID for me has been more time at home, allowing me to be more consistent with exercise. Being home more has also allowed me to invest more time into practicing yoga and meditation, both of which I also enjoy.

When people ask me how I find time to exercise, I always tell them that I don't think exercise costs me much, if any, time. In fact, often it seems that for every hour spent exercising, I get two to three hours back in not only energy but also mental and emotional vitality. Exercise and self-care are investments with huge returns.

Choices

When my daughters Erin and Amanda were growing up, I would tell them, "Life is full of choices, make good ones."

Growing up in both church and Christian school, my favorite chapter of the Bible was and still is Deuteronomy 30. Some think that is a strange chapter to be someone's favorite, but I like how Moses makes the choices in front of the Israelites crystal clear. You may recall that at the time Deuteronomy was recorded, Moses had led the Israelites out of Egypt and was at the end of his life. In his last speech to the people, Moses told them that if they made the right choices, they would be blessed. As I told my daughters, life is about choices.

In the classic *Man's Search for Meaning*, Victor Frankl shares his story as a Jew in German concentration camps before his eventual release by allied soldiers. Writing in one of the most influential books ever written, Frankl argues that everything can be taken away from a person other than his or her ability to decide how they will view their situation, and it is an extremely powerful lesson. A lesser-known, but I believe equally impactful book, *The Choice* by Edith Eger, covers similar ground. Eger also writes about her experience as a Jew in Hitler's concentration camps where her parents were both killed by the Nazis. She writes about the decades that followed her concentration camp experience, sharing a compelling story of how she eventually decided to focus on what she had, not what she had lost.

As leaders, we have a lot of choices to make that will have a significant impact on both us and our teams. Make sure those choices you make are the best they could possibly be.

Conclusion

The purpose of *Education of a CEO* is to help those who want to be better leaders by sharing my experiences over nearly four decades. I have been incredibly blessed with opportunities to learn in many ways, and I don't take that for granted. My hope is that sharing some of my "education" will help others. If it helps even one leader, it will be worth the time invested in writing this book.

As we conclude, there are four more quick things that are important to share.

Be an Inspiration

It is imperative that leaders inspire their teams, and this book's original outline included a chapter on becoming an inspirational leader. As I sat to write that chapter, however, it became obvious that the stories I was going to share about inspiring a team were already in the book.

My thinking crystalized around the idea that there is not a to-do list leaders can check off to become inspirational. Leaders who have true character, competency, and chemistry inspire.

Finally, I realized that inspiration is what this entire book is about: Leaders who do the right things, treat people well, and inspire.

There Is No Silver Bullet

Speaking to groups around the world and meeting with leaders who have asked for my advice, I have made one consistent observation. Leaders who aspire to improve are often looking for a quick fix or what is sometimes called a silver bullet. Generally, they believe they are doing well and are just one secret ingredient away from being an impactful, results-achieving leader. That is rarely, if ever, true.

If there is a leadership silver bullet, I have yet to find it.

Being an effective leader is a never-ending quest that includes working to understand and implement all the various topics we have covered in this book. Of course, a leader will often see quick results by implementing one or two easy changes, but to reach your true potential, you must take a holistic approach, and that requires work.

Knowledge vs. Execution

Many times, I have been contacted by a leader who has tried something new and given up, saying something like, "It sounded like a good idea, but it didn't work for me."

There is a big difference in knowing what to do and being able to execute what you know to do. Don't think that knowing what to do means you will execute it well the first time. Oftentimes, you won't.

Implementation is much harder than knowing. Execution is an effort to apply knowledge with a group of people who have different experiences and trust levels.

Effective execution of the ideas presented in this book almost always requires trust among the team. Once again, a great starting place to build trust among your team is having them read and discuss the book *5 Dysfunctions of a Team* by Patrick Lencioni.

Even after building trust, execution also takes a lot of effort and a willingness to fail.

Be a Learner

I will finish where I started: Be a learner.

The closest thing there is to a silver bullet in leadership is being a learner. If you are a true learner, it will almost certainly lead to success.

Good luck. I look forward to hearing success stories from your "education."

Appendix

Recommended Books

As most readers of this book likely picked up on already, I enjoy reading. I also enjoy recommending books to those who are interested.

I will start the list with other books I have written, which can be easily found online.

What Would Dad Say? Is a book I wrote with my friend David Nelms after both of our fathers had died too young. It is a fictional discussion between a father who is now in heaven and his son, who is still living on earth.

Yeargin on Management is a compilation of over a hundred articles I have published. It does not include all my articles but will give the reader a good feel for the many management and leadership topics I have shared thoughts on in the past twenty-five years.

Making Life Better: The Correct Craft Story is a history of the company where I serve as CEO. In this book, I write about both Correct Craft's history before I arrived and the exciting growth we have experienced since 2006. This book also extensively covers the organizational values that make Correct Craft unique.

Some of the business books that have impacted my thinking are the following:

Probably the book I have most recommended over the past twenty-five years is **The Seven Habits of Highly Effective People** by

Stephen R. Covey. If I could only recommend one business book, this would probably be it.

All of Patrick Lencioni's books will make your organization better. If I had to read only three of them, in order, they would be **Five Dysfunctions of a Team, The Advantage, and The Motive**. Interestingly, several years ago, I sat next to Pat on a flight from Orlando to Salt Lake City, and he was a really nice guy.

Abundance and **The Future Is Faster Than You Think** were written by Peter Diamandis, and both books will blow your mind. The next ten years will bring dramatic change, and Diamandis lays it out clearly and succinctly. He also makes an argument that the future will bring tremendous disruption to current businesses, with newcomers creating new business models. However, overall, he is very optimistic about the future abundance technology will create.

The late Harvard professor Clayton Christenson wrote his classic **The Innovator's Dilemma** to explain why most companies go out of business rather than disruptively innovate. This happens even though the companies can easily adopt technologies that eventually put them out of business. Anyone who runs a business needs to read this book; it is a matter of survival.

Six Thinking Hats by Edward de Bono presents a great tool for seeing all sides of an issue. This book helps people significantly improve their decision-making.

Jim Collins' classic **Good to Great** helps companies understand the difference between being just good and being great.

Each year, I pick a subject that I want to learn about, and one year, I committed a few months to studying negotiation. Some good books I read during that time were **Never Split the Difference** by Chris Voss, **Negotiation Genius** by Malhotra and Bazerman, **Getting to Yes** by Roger Fisher and William Ury, **Getting More** by Stuart Diamond, **Influence: The Psychology of Persuasion** by Robert

Cialdini, **Crucial Conversations** by various authors, and **Negotiating the Impossible** by Deepak Malhotra.

The Goal is a classic operations management book by Eliyahu Goldratt. Definitely listen to the audiobook version of this one; it is acted out by various readers, which makes it very interesting.

If you run any kind of organization, read Simon Sinek's **Start with Why**. This book has had a huge impact on me and our company.

Brothers Chip and Dan Heath have written two outstanding books. The first is The **Power of Moments,** and the second is my favorite book on dealing with change, **Switch**.

When by Daniel Pink is an outstanding book on the importance of timing.

The Undoing Project by Michael Lewis and **Thinking Fast and Slow** by Daniel Kahneman were two books that introduced me to behavioral economics, a concept that significantly improved my thinking.

Speaking of behavioral economics, other great books on the topic include **Misbehaving** by Nobel prize winner Richard Thaler, **Nudge** by Thaler and Cass Sunstein, and **Predictably Irrational** by Dan Ariely.

In **Measure What Matters**, John Doerr shows how focusing on the right things can help any organization drive results.

Henry Cloud, in his excellent book **Necessary Endings,** explains why it is a mistake to hold onto things we should let go. This is a must-read for every leader.

In **This Time Is Different,** Reinhart and Rogoff explain how we consistently ignore the past in a way that leads to unnecessary trouble.

Yvon Chouinard, Founder of Patagonia, explains how a company can be both very high performing and socially responsible. Even a leader who defines social responsibility differently that Chouinard can learn a lot from ***Let My People Go Surfing.***

Building a Story Brand explains how to use stories to create a powerful marketing message. It's written by New York Times bestselling author Donald Miller.

Successful Wall Street investor Nassim Taleb writes how rare and unpredictable events can change our world and how standard forecasting consistently fails organizations in his classic, ***The Black Swan.***

The Halo Effect by Phil Rosenzweig explains how even the most seasoned business leaders get hijacked by delusions based on results they misunderstand. The book helps leaders understand the difference between fact and fiction and better understand what is really driving results.

The Culture Map by international business expert Erin Meyer explains how to do business across various cultures. For a company like ours that operates in about seventy countries, this book is valuable.

Before doing business in Russia, ***Red Notice*** by Bill Browder is a must read. This true story reads like a fast-paced novel as Browder writes about his real-life adventures, some pretty scary, doing business in Russia.

In another true story that reads like a page-turning novel, John Carreyrou explains in ***Bad Blood*** how a college dropout became the world's richest self-made woman. At one point, she had a net worth of many billions of dollars by conning some of the nation's most reputable leaders and then eventually lost it all.

Thinking in Bets by professional poker player Annie Duke does a great job of explaining how most of our most important decisions are not clear choices—they are a matter of managing probabilities.

Harvard professors Douglas Stone and Sheila Heen in their excellent book, ***Thanks for the Feedback***, not only explain why getting feedback on all we do is important but also describe how we can accept it in a way that benefits us the most.

The Billionaire Who Wasn't by Conor O'Clery is the compelling story of Chuck Feeney who made billions through duty-free stores and gave it away during his own life. As I write this, Feeney is eighty-nine and living in a San Francisco apartment after giving away all his money.

Dee Ann Turner, former Vice President of Talent at Chick-fil-A, wrote a great book on people and culture called ***Bet on Talent***.

Leadership and Self Deception by The Arbinger Institute helps its readers understand how we can all be so self-deceived.

Speak of being self-deceived, nobody explains that better than Kathryn Schulz in her excellent book ***Being Wrong***.

Mindset by Carol Dweck is an absolute must-read. It is impossible to be a great leader without a growth mindset.

How to Win Friends and Influence People by Dale Carnegie was written decades ago but is still helpful for those looking to better manage interpersonal relationships.

Any leader who achieves success must read ***Derailed*** by Tim Irwin. Irwin does a great job explaining where successful leaders go wrong.

Rebel Talent by Harvard professor Francesca Gino shares how having rebels on your team can help improve results. She also helped me understand the importance of building on a team's strengths. I have taken a couple classes with Francesca and always learn a lot from her.

In his book **_Triggers_**, the world's most sought-after executive coach, Marshall Goldsmith, shares the best ways to change behaviors that are holding us back using lessons learned from coaching the top leaders of Fortune 500 companies. In the book, Goldsmith shares advice top leaders pay hundreds of thousands of dollars to hear from him personally.

About the Author

Bill Yeargin is the CEO of Correct Craft. Under Bill's leadership, Correct Craft has won all their industry's major awards and developed a unique culture of "Making Life Better." A passionate lifelong learner, Bill earned an MBA and has completed post-graduate education at Harvard, Stanford, Villanova, Wharton, and MIT.

He served both the Obama and Trump administrations on cabinet-level advisory councils and *Florida Trend* magazine recognized Bill as one of "Florida's Most Influential Business Leaders."

Bill has been published hundreds of times, has authored four books including the best-seller ***Making Life Better: The Correct Craft Story***, and is a sought-after conference speaker.

He and his wife Leigh have two daughters, Erin (married to Ben) and Amanda.

CPSIA information can be obtained
at www.ICGtesting.com
Printed in the USA
BVHW041914250222
629686BV00003B/5/J